CONFIDENT
BY CHOICE

CONFIDENT
BY CHOICE

THE
THREE SMALL DECISIONS
THAT BUILD EVERYDAY
COURAGE

JUAN BENDAÑA

BALLANTINE BOOKS

NEW YORK

Ballantine Books
An imprint of Random House
A division of Penguin Random House LLC
1745 Broadway, New York, NY 10019
randomhousebooks.com
penguinrandomhouse.com

Hardcover ISBN 978-0-593-72561-0
Ebook ISBN 978-0-593-72562-7

Printed in the United States of America on acid-free paper

1st Printing

FIRST EDITION

BOOK TEAM: Production editor: *Michelle Daniel* • Managing editor:
Pamela Alders • Production manager: *Maggie Hart* • Copy editor:
Sue Warga • Proofreaders: *Melissa Churchill, Cathy Sangermano*

Book design by Barbara M. Bachman

The authorized representative in the EU for product safety and
compliance is Penguin Random House Ireland, Morrison Chambers,
32 Nassau Street, Dublin D02 YH68, Ireland.
https://eu-contact.penguin.ie

To my wife, Gabriela,
who believed in me more than
I believed in myself.
I wouldn't be the person I am today
without you by my side.

Contents

———

INTRODUCTION:
You Can Build Confidence ix

CHAPTER 1: Confidence Is a Verb   3

CHAPTER 2: One Ounce at a Time   20

DECISION #1:
Micro-Energy 45

CHAPTER 3: The Five Micro-Energy Boosters   47

CHAPTER 4: How to Overcome the
Five Energy Killers   69

DECISION #2:
Micro-Courage 89

CHAPTER 5: "I'm Not There, *Yet*"   91

CHAPTER 6: The Opponents   108

DECISION #3:
Micro-Action   133

CHAPTER 7: Baby Steps Only   135

CHAPTER 8: Ten Micro-Actions   154

RESULT:
Micro-Proof   167

CHAPTER 9: You Succeed (Even When You Fail)   169

CHAPTER 10: From Micro-Proof to Identity Shift   185

CONCLUSION:
Time to Open the Door   199

Acknowledgments   201
Notes   203
Index   209

Introduction

___

You Can Build Confidence

I S IT POSSIBLE TO *BUILD* CONFIDENCE?

We know how to build muscle, grow flowers, or bake a cake. We know that if we go to the gym, water the plants, or follow the recipe, we can create what we want. We can start with small muscles, a few seeds, or a pile of ingredients, and with the right actions, a little practice, and enough time, we can transform those beginnings into powerful endings.

But is that true with self-confidence? Can we wake up and decide that we want more self-confidence, then follow a series of steps that will predictably *develop* more of the confidence that we wish we had?

I'm happy to tell you, *yes.* Science, countless stories, and plenty of evidence prove it.

But I get it if you don't believe me. I didn't, either. Until I did.

___

GRINGO JUAN

___

"SOME PEOPLE WERE born with the gift of communication. You were not."

Just in case I was developing any wild ideas about one day becoming a professional communicator, the words of my high school English teacher, Mrs. H., were always there to remind me of who I wasn't—a gifted speaker. That was a real shame, because I was already running low on confidence that I would grow into a successful adult.

Long before Mrs. H. offered her unsolicited diagnosis on my future speaking abilities, medical doctors had noted I had a running problem. More precisely, a *not*-running problem. Whenever I would try to get my feet moving faster than a brisk pace, I'd get an awful pain in my side that would take over my body. No one could figure out the cause of the pain, so after multiple clinic visits, the practitioners told me that whenever I felt pain while running, I should pause *immediately*, because otherwise something "really bad" would happen. By the time I was a teenager, I was the best 400-meter walker around. Becoming a professional athlete was never on the table.

What I lacked in speed I made up for in extra weight. Not a lot, but enough for my dad to say: "*Juan, estás gordo y no hay nada peor en el mundo*"—Juan, you're fat, and there's nothing worse you could be, in the whole world.

Why did he say it in Spanish? Well, that brings me to my ethnic and national identity crisis.

I'm Nicaraguan Canadian, and I don't look anything like what you or anyone else probably imagines: I'm tall with green eyes, brownish-blond hair, and light skin. I get it—that doesn't sound bad at all in certain Western circles. In fact, if my name were John Baker, those features would likely be an advantage. But my name's not John Baker. It's Juan Bendaña. So when I was growing up, even my family questioned my ethnicity. I was commonly called *chele*—Spanish slang for a fair-skinned Nicaraguan—which to me was not an endearing term; rather, it was a constant reminder that I wasn't a "real" Nicaraguan. And only those Nicaraguans who knew me well called me *chele*. Most locals in Nicaragua still call me *gringo* to this day, mistaking me for an American tourist. Back in Canada, where I grew up, I often heard similar insults; when I was a kid, people constantly mispronounced (and made fun of) my name, often vocalizing the common assumption that I was adopted. I'd learned one thing by the time I got to high school—how to fit in, a lesson I'd learned by necessity. In middle school, my weight, light skin, and oddly high-pitched voice had attracted all the wrong attention. I got beaten up for no apparent reason, received death threats from the school's biggest bully, and heard plenty of lesser abuse, such as:

- "Go back to Nicaragua."
- "You're adopted."
- "What kind of white guy is named Juan?"
- "No one likes you."
- "You're a waste of time."

To protect myself from not fitting neatly into any one category, I learned to fit in just enough in *every* category. What started as a defense mechanism soon became a popularity tool. The right words, the right clothes, and *snap*—I'd be hanging with the drama club kids. A few changes to my personality, and the jocks from the teams I could never join were inviting me over after school. I didn't care much for photography, but the photography kids liked me. I didn't know how to break-dance, but I hung with the breakers. It seemed that if I'd learned *anything* in school, it was how to communicate to the world that I was exactly what they wanted me to be. In fact, in drama class, an essentially communication-based environment, I earned my only good grade. That's why it had particularly stung when Mrs. H. criticized my communication skills. So, I tried to brush off her words, and I got back to "fitting in."

And then I met *her*.

She was the beautiful blond cheerleader I thought Gringo Juan could never date. Naturally, I fell hard and fast. And you know what? She reciprocated! We planned our whole future life together: We knew what city we would move to, what kind of house we wanted, the breed of dog we'd own, the car we'd drive. And then, when I was twenty, that relationship suddenly ended . . . and with it went any last shred of confidence I had. Suddenly, the camouflage that was covering up for the bullied, overweight kid vanished, and my real lack of confidence surfaced. After my girlfriend and I broke up, I withdrew from the world. I stopped attending college classes, I refused to leave my house, and many days I didn't even get out of bed. What had been a little extra snacking suddenly turned into a binge-eating disorder and I ballooned, seemingly overnight. When food failed to provide enough comfort, I found alcohol. First, it was just Friday nights, but then, I added in Saturdays. Soon, I was drinking all the way into Tuesday nights to numb the dissatisfaction with my life. This four- to five-night drinking eventually landed me in a hospital-bound ambulance for alcohol poisoning. I was a twentysomething with no future, no girl, and now—at seventy-five pounds overweight—medically obese. My lack of confidence had given way to a totally broken person.

Little did I know that a phone call was about to not only

save my life, but teach me how to gain confidence, even if it wasn't something I was born with. Confidence, I would soon learn, is a skill set, one that anybody—even obese, bullied, depressed Gringo Juan—can use to change their own life.

THE FRESH START THAT FELT LIKE A SLOW START

"HEY, JUAN! WHY don't you come out to California for a bit and crash on my couch? It seems like you could use a fresh start."

I'd always liked Luis. Not only was he an outstanding friend, but he was also many of the things I wasn't: naturally great with people (he spoke for a living), a fantastic communicator (he published a bestselling book the year I visited him), and—seemingly—naturally confident. So I hopped on a plane to Los Angeles.

Sleeping on Luis's couch, I had an up-close picture of his life: an early riser, a gym-head, a personal and professional coach. His weeks usually involved some sort of speaking engagement (my dream!). His professional talents seemed to flow from his natural self-confidence, the kind I didn't have. Oddly, a lot of the ups and downs in his life seemed similar to mine: His teachers had told him he'd never amount to much, he'd been diagnosed with a medical condition (ADD), and he would have flunked out of high school except that his English teacher was so tired of him, she gave him a D-minus just to pass him so she never had to see him again. And yet here he was coaching business leaders, being interviewed by media outlets, and offering his expertise to the world. Obviously, he must have been born with confidence, right? I asked him about it.

"Early on, I didn't have a lot of confidence, but the more I focused on what I wanted, the more energy I had to pursue my goals."

"But what about the hard days?" I asked.

"I lean *into* discomfort and take action. The results provide the proof that I should keep going."

At that moment, Luis couldn't have known that he'd just planted the seeds of the Confidence Cycle. Honestly, I didn't, either. I barely understood much of what he was saying. But I was broke, girlfriend-less, overweight, and sleeping on his couch, while he lived a beautiful life much like the one I'd always wanted. Why not try it his way? I'd understood at least this much from what he said: Find some energy and take some action. So, I went for it. I was already feeling pretty pumped from my talk with Luis and my new California environment, which helped give me an initial boost. I also made a list of the changes I wanted to see in my life. As a bonus, for the next few months, I'd be face-to-face with Luis, who'd experienced some of the same struggles as I had, apparently *wasn't* born confident, and still managed to live the life I wanted. I used all this as my new daily inspiration.

At first, I tried to make sweeping changes, but I didn't make big progress. In fact, I mostly just failed. For instance, I tried waking up early. I remember setting *four alarms,* for 6:00 A.M., 6:02, 6:05, and 6:09, and *still* waking up past ten. I made professional goals like "send fifty emails to network contacts," and then found myself staring at the computer screen for an hour. Once, even after I had "eat a healthy meal" on my day's list of challenges, instead I ate pizza. Not *some* pizza, a *whole* pizza.

But I kept trying. And little by little, I saw something change. One of the major differences was that *this* go-around,

I was staring my self-limiting beliefs right in the face. Each time after I failed (or almost failed), I'd hear the same old voices in my head:

- "You've never been able to lose weight."
- "You're not going to stick to this."
- "You might as well quit."
- "You're a loser."

But now, I felt something new. Inspired by Luis's instructions to push through discomfort, I navigated past this noise. I reminded myself that just taking action was proof I was moving in the right direction, and that idea kept fueling me forward, even through failure.

Once I got home from that trip, I had a little momentum. I hadn't changed all that much, but I (sort of) had a game plan—I would focus on what I wanted, even if it was scary; (probably) fail; then try again. Knowing that the first step of the game was to find something that inspired me or made me feel more alive—what Luis had called "energy"—was really helpful.

I started smaller, focusing on the tiny changes that I believed would lead to outsized results. I tried to wake up earlier, do a small (maybe thirty-minute) workout, then come home. I tried to send ten emails, then read something inspirational, then send ten more emails. As long as I kept moving, I *felt* like I was heading in the right direction.

Luis had taught me that if I could add some energy into my life, I'd be able to start a cycle that would lead to proof. Every time I accomplished something small, *or even tried,* that was enough proof to spark something positive inside me: *At least you tried, Juan!* And that started a new cycle—try again. With enough energy to keep getting up, and enough proof to keep creating energy, I made small gains.

It was hard. It was messy. I failed constantly. There were periods of over six months when I didn't feel any sort of change in my life. But I could tell that, overall, something *was* working, which gave me confidence. Knowing that it was OK to feel discomfort and then push through it made me feel like trying again, even if it was painful. Understanding that I'd often want to give up but that finding some new energy as a spark was the first step—not just magically conjuring confidence itself—made me feel more alive.

JUAN BECOMES A SPEAKER

I COMMITTED TO following the same pattern—find energy, take action, (probably) fail, and start again. One major area I focused on was becoming a professional speaker. This had been a dream of mine since I was twelve years old. Using what I'd learned—to start with energy—I began by practicing two hours a day. Then I built a website. I had no coding experience, but I gave it a shot. Once it was up and running, I felt even prouder of what I'd done. Then I started sending emails to event planners within a five-hour drive of Toronto, Canada.

After two weeks and thirty-five hours of emailing, I landed my first speaking gig: seven people in a student group at the University of Toronto. I was even getting paid. The speaking fee? A coffee mug. And I was *pumped*.

Getting that gig was the energy boost I needed to ramp up my commitment and take even more action. I sent more emails. Got more rejections, then more rejections, but *then . . .*

another gig! Then another, and another. Wins started to compound on each other. Before I knew it, I was a *professional
speaker.*

———

EIGHT YEARS AFTER my visit with Luis, I sat in a coffee shop.
By then, each little win that had started in Luis's living room
had compounded, exponentially, to create a new person. I'd
lost so much weight that some people didn't recognize me. I
felt fully comfortable in my name and my own skin. I was also
what I'd always dreamed of, a professional speaker (doing the
very thing Mrs. H. had said I could never do): I was fully sup-
porting myself with speaking engagements across North
America, delivering keynotes at Fortune 500 companies about
leadership and peak performance.

As I sat there sipping coffee, I asked myself the question
anyone would have asked: *How did I get here?* How had self-
conscious, bullied, seventy-five-pounds-overweight Gringo
Juan become a top international speaker for companies like
American Express, Sony Pictures, and Disney? As a kid, I'd
had no confidence—zero, none, nada. Even the small amount
I'd gained in high school had vanished after my breakup. But
now, as an adult, I somehow had the confidence to speak in
front of thousands of leaders. I wasn't thinking about all this
to impress myself. I actually wanted an answer: *How* had I
gone from zero confidence to plenty of it?

I started charting out the last decade of my life as if it was
a giant story (and, as we'll discuss later, all our lives *are* stories!). When I got back to the plot point of Luis's living
room—where my unlikely transformation had started—I noticed something.

Luis had showed me that he was living out his confidence in exactly the reverse order most of us do—he took action, watched the proof develop, and then allowed confidence to grow as a result of his decisions. But I'd always viewed my life's relationship with confidence with the opposite perspective, the same way you've probably always seen it: My initial confidence level sort of dictated what actions I'd take.

What's more, I was never in control of my self-confidence; it just sort of bubbled up as a mix of my environment, how popular I was, and what I believed other people thought about me. Throw all that into a mix, and a sort of confidence score pops out: As bullied, overweight Gringo Juan, I had low confidence. When I learned how to be a chameleon in high school to achieve a little more popularity, I had higher confidence. When I landed my dream girl, I was at (what I thought was) the top of my confidence game. When she left, I was destroyed. On and on, point for confidence, point for self-doubt. Until my talk with Luis, my confidence had been nothing more than a walking scoreboard.

But Luis had shown me that *confidence is a result of decisions and actions, not just a starting point.* Then, perhaps without even realizing it, Luis had handed me the beginnings of a system to *develop* confidence with my decisions: He'd shown me that you must first find enough **ENERGY**, then muster **COURAGE** to face the discomfort, taking **ACTION** to move past it, which will give you **PROOF** that you at least did something. That proof then gives you a new spark of energy, beginning the cycle again. *That's it!* I thought, sitting there at the coffee table, doodling in my journal. I looked at every area of my life, and I could see that same cycle Luis had originally offered me, occurring again and again:

How had I lost weight? I'd found some energy by thinking of what I'd feel like after I went to the gym, mustered the courage to face the discomforting thoughts (*Juan, you'll never lose weight*), then took action, and voilà—I had proof, not always of weight loss itself, but at least that I'd gone to the gym even as someone who was overweight. That proof gave me a boost of energy, which started the cycle again.

I could see the same cycle functioning in every area of my life that I'd improved: When I wanted to be a professional speaker, even without any gigs, I started the same way: I could see the website I'd set up for my professional speaking career, which gave me some energy about my potential future opportunities. From there, I found the courage to face the discomfort of contacting people out of the blue. Then, I took action by emailing them, which provided enough proof that I could email people and make an ask. That proof was enough motivation for me to start the cycle again. Eventually, of course, someone did say "yes," which gave me even more energy.

On and on, in example after example, I saw the same thing—energy, courage, action, proof, repeat.

For the next week, this cycle lived rent-free in my head. I couldn't stop thinking about it. At my next speaking gig, I interrupted myself midway through my talk and said, "I'm so sorry, but I have a new idea that I have to tell you all about. I think I found the secret to building confidence!" I shared it, and the crowd was ecstatic. Not because I'm brilliant, but because the simplicity rang so true, and it was so easy to get started. I remember a doctoral student, who had been writing her dissertation on leadership, was sitting in the back of the room. After the presentation, she approached me, started asking all sorts of scientific questions, and told me this was the most exciting, simplest idea on confidence she'd ever heard. I started sharing the idea with others at my presentations. Then I started posting it online. I refined the wording and the cycle. I tested it with my coaching clients. And it worked. I remember one young lady, Daysha, who built confidence in a moment using what I now call the Confidence Cycle. I was delivering a keynote to an emerging-leaders conference in Texas. Daysha was sitting in the front row. She'd been nervous before coming into the conference: She'd recently started her career and was looking to become an integral part of this new industry, so she wanted to make a good impression with her peers and potential colleagues. At the presentation, I talked about the importance of building confidence at the beginning of one's career. I unpacked the Confidence Cycle, and we specifically discussed self-limiting beliefs. During the question-and-answer portion, Daysha shot her hand up. But, then, just as quickly, she pulled it down, as if her hand had gone up by instinct, not intention.

"Thank you so much for volunteering to be first!" I said to her.

I could see her nervous thoughts as if they were in bubbles floating above her head: *What if I ask a stupid question? What if I stumble over a word? Am I really the person who should be asking a question right now?*

I interrupted the silent conversation by asking, "What's your name?"

"Daysha."

"It looked like you were going to ask something. What belief made you pull your hand back down?"

"That what I have to say doesn't really matter."

"Is that really true?"

"No," she said slowly.

"OK," I said. "We all have self-limiting beliefs. But in terms of the Confidence Cycle, you already shot your hand up, and that proved something, right?"

She thought for a moment before answering, "It proved that I can put myself out there, even before I'm ready."

"Yup. Where else could you use that same mentality?"

"In my career . . . or my relationships . . . or with new people that I meet . . ."

She got on a roll, and I couldn't stop her. By the end, she was pouring out ideas on what could happen in her life if she applied the same principles to other areas: If she made a decision first, then allowed those decisions to build her confidence, she could create the life and self-image she wanted.

Daysha's face lit up. She saw (in real time) the power of the Confidence Cycle at work:

- **ENERGY.** Because she was initially eager to ask a question, she'd shot her hand up instinctually.
- **COURAGE.** She felt uncomfortable after I called her out, but she found a moment of courage to have a conversation anyway.
- **ACTION.** She went ahead and shared, even though she was scared.
- **PROOF.** Toward the end of my conversation with Daysha, I asked the crowd, "How many of you already like Daysha and would want to be her friend?" The room erupted. All of that, of course, gave Daysha proof, providing more energy to start the cycle again in other areas of her life.

Today, Daysha owns the room in every circle she walks into. The shy newcomer is gone, and she got there by taking a simple step forward. More than a decade later, I've now delivered presentations to more than three hundred thousand people in venues of all sizes, from rooms of seven to stadiums of thirty thousand. I've now worked with Fortune 100 companies such as American Express and Disney and have coached actors, Olympians, and CEOs, helping them build what I struggled with for the better part of my life: confidence. And if there's one thing I've learned—which has been confirmed by science—it's this: Confidence can be built.

This book will show you how. We are going to break down the step-by-step process that you can take to create the life you want.

———

THE BOOK YOU'RE holding is about the self-limiting beliefs that have created invisible but entirely real barriers between you and what you want—between the small life that you may have confined yourself to and the beautiful, amazing life just waiting for you outside an unlocked door. In what areas of your life have you allowed limiting beliefs to hold you back? Maybe you have brilliant ideas that could make big changes in your workplace, but often, just before you share them with your team, your boss, or your department, something tells you to stay quiet. Maybe you're a stay-at-home parent who wants to start a business, but just before you take the next step to pursue your plan, something inside you says, *Stop! That's not for you!* Or maybe your battle is in the relationship department. Perhaps once you get a couple of months into a romance, you tense up, thinking you don't deserve a great partner, so you make up all sorts of reasons you two can't be together. You could have doubts regarding school, fitness, parenting, finances, travel, or all those areas at once. We all have inner pain—psychological turbulence that shows up at exactly the wrong time, just as we start to pick up speed in the race of life. The pain (and the voices) may show up halfway through soccer practice, six months into a relationship, or ten minutes into a meeting, but you know what I'm talking about. For most of us, when a voice tells us to retreat to what's comfortable, to stop moving forward, to halt growth, we listen. We allow that voice to steal the one thing we need to move forward in every area of our life: *confidence.*

What if everything you want to be—a self-confident person at work, a loving husband and a terrific father, a great friend, a fantastic writer, the lady who knows how to ask for the promotion she deserves—is available to you, just on the other side of that discomfort? What if you've been shrinking back your whole life for no real reason, except that a voice told you that you had to slow down?

If you've been holding yourself back because of a lack of confidence, then that, my friends, is living in a prison with an unlocked door—a place that feels as if it's inescapable, but in reality, it's one you can walk out of at any time.

With more confidence, some of us would ask for the promotion we've deserved for years. Others would finally launch that company we've always wanted to build. Maybe you'd finally ask that special person out. Maybe, with a little more confidence, you'd have the self-respect to *end* a relationship. For all of us, things would be just a bit better. I bet you can think of one area, right now, where, with more confidence, you'd improve:

- "With more confidence, I'd be a better spouse."
- "With more confidence, I'd be a better teacher."
- "With more confidence, I'd be a better manager."
- "With more confidence, I'd be a better _____."

Even if you don't believe me (yet) that confidence can be built, you picked up this book for a reason. You have a _____ that you're trying to improve. Whatever *your* _____ is, I want you to find the confidence that you need to get there.

Gyms are useful places, because they help everyone, regardless of where each person starts, to build the muscle they want to have. People walk into the same gym from a variety of different starting points. I've been to the same gym and seen real-life Olympic athletes using the same equipment as those who were trying to shed fifty pounds. Others are just trying to stay toned. But the same equipment, the same process, can help any of them. What if confidence was like a muscle?

In this book, I want to give you the right equipment, instructions, and process that have helped build self-confidence for thousands of executives, rising stars, and stay-at-home parents.

Whatever goes in your _____, we're going to fill it.

It's time to elevate our confidence.

CONFIDENT
BY CHOICE

1.

Confidence Is a Verb

———

I'm proof that people aren't born with talent. If you listen to my early recordings, I can't play guitar and I can't really sing or write music very well either. It's all come through practice; everything comes through practice. You start off with a little spark, and it's whether or not you nurture that spark. You have to expand it and work on it.

—ED SHEERAN

EVERY GOOD STORY HAS AN EPIC BATTLE. ONE THE HERO wins.

You're obviously the hero. And since you're reading a book about confidence, you could easily assume that overcoming a lack of confidence will be your epic battle. You might be right. But here's where you're wrong: The antidote to a lack of confidence isn't just more confidence.

While adding more of something often works to make things better (in Canada, we top pancakes, waffles, crepes, oats, and ice cream with maple syrup; if it doesn't taste quite right at first, just add a bit more maple), that doesn't cut it here. That's because the confidence struggle is a little bit trickier than simply adding more. Let's break it down.

Researchers have been trying to unlock self-confidence, self-esteem, self-efficacy, and similar topics for decades. They relate the concepts to sports performance, leadership performance, academic performance, ability to learn . . . you name it, they've studied it. There's almost no topic smart people won't try to relate self-confidence to; in 2021, researchers studied three hundred Romanian employees, trying to figure out how their self-confidence related to their ability to utilize e-learning.[1]

But we don't need a bunch of academic studies to tell us what we already know about confidence: We all want more of it.

Most of us believe that if we just had more confidence, we'd be bolder in our workplaces, be happier in our relationships, and achieve our goals more frequently. We envy the person who seems to have all the necessary confidence to speak up when they feel mistreated, or to ask for what they really want in life.

But the problem, or so we think, is that confidence wasn't ever granted to us. When the Confidence Genie went around handing out various amounts of this magical trait, he seemed somehow to have skipped us, or at least not to have been as generous as we would have liked. Most of us walk around believing that we're stuck with the amount of confidence granted to us at birth. If our confidence does change, it's only because someone else validated (or invalidated) our beliefs about ourselves:

- We ask someone on a date, and they say yes: point for self-confidence
- We get fired from our job: point for self-doubt
- Our boss gives us a raise: point for self-confidence

Overall, most of us start out with a bit of self-confidence (which is inevitably less than we would have liked), and then we walk around with a giant scoreboard keeping a tally in our minds.

Points for Self-Confidence	Points for Self-Doubt
Promotion at work	Going through a breakup
Getting a second date	Getting fired from your job
Being hired for a new job	Being rejected
Receiving positive feedback	Failing at your goal
Crushing a presentation at work	People laughing at you
Having friends laugh at a joke	Tripping over your words during a meeting

All these points add up to what we believe is our self-confidence score. Of course, there *are* some people who seem to have total control over their confidence (just not us). Those people, though, generally seem to be the perfect size, with perfect teeth and perfect hair. They always know what to say and when to say it. They have the perfect spouse, the perfect job, the perfect friends. When the Confidence Genie visited them, he granted an extra dose of everything, from physical attributes to communication skills to having a super-cool job. Their confidence started out great and only went up from there as the world congratulated them on their undeserved merits. Glen Powell. These people are Glen Powell.

But you know the problem with that philosophy of happenstance?

It's just not true.

I want you to pay attention to the next story. It's a story

about someone who has all the confidence in the world, but (at least when they started out) they shouldn't have had any confidence—unless we've all been wrong about self-confidence from the beginning.

———

FIFTY MILLION RECORDS.[2] Twenty-seven billion views on You-Tube.[3] Four Grammys.[4] Taylor Swift's trusted confidant. A guy all the girls seem to want.

On one hand, there couldn't be a better picture of confidence than Ed Sheeran—the guy who bravely raps onstage with his lovely accent, his loop pedal, and his hair blowing in the wind. But on the other hand, we have Ed Sheeran before he was, well, *Ed Sheeran*—a scruffy, red-haired, lazy-eyed, couch-surfing, stuttering, broke musician wannabe. If *that* guy can be confident and wind up an all-star, so can you.

Pay attention to his story, because you'll notice that at every juncture he is given a reason not to be confident, but then he *does* something that turns the corner.

Sheeran was born in 1991, with a birthmark on his eye. When doctors tried to surgically remove it a few years later, they inadvertently created both a lazy eye and a stutter.[5] Combine those with his ginger hair, and you can imagine what primary school was like for him. In one interview, he said "cried every day" before going.[6]

Now, that could have been the beginning of a really, really sad story. But it turns out it was the beginning of an incredible one. To help him get over his stutter—which speech therapy sessions couldn't seem to cure—his uncle bought him an Eminem album, which nine-year-old Sheeran latched on to, teaching himself to rap every lyric. Miraculously, the rapping cured his stutter.

At sixteen he dropped out of school and moved to London, without his parents, to start pursuing his career in music. Did he get invited by the gods of music? Did Michael Jackson come back from the dead to tell Sheeran he would one day smash Jackson's concert records? No. Sheeran simply made a *choice:* "I was s*** scared when I first went to London. But it was just something I knew I had to do."

Sheeran quickly figured out the trick to music—hard work. He knew that everyone with a guitar was trying to play at least one gig every week. So Sheeran did one almost every night; his first year, he performed *three hundred* shows.

By seventeen, he was gaining a bit of local renown, and industry "experts" started telling him to stop using his loop pedal, to stop rapping, and to turn his songs into techno ditties. Sheeran listened at first, but he soon took his own route. He didn't enjoy techno and he liked rapping (so did his small group of fans), so he decided to do it his way, continuing to be the authentic ginger-haired rapper-singer-songwriter that he was. "I [didn't] care anymore. I just want[ed] to play songs that I enjoy[ed]."[7]

A couple of years later, in 2009, he met a young lady named Angel. She'd been living on the streets off and on, and a charity offered her a place to stay for the Christmas season; she met Sheeran when he did a show at that homeless shelter. Based on her life, he wrote the international hit "The A Team." That song, based on Angel's story, became part of *his* story and even made history—going seven times platinum in the United States, and multi-platinum in almost a dozen other countries.

With "The A Team" blasting across radio stations around the world, he was propelled into fame. To date, he's sold more than 150 million records, set the record for the highest-grossing concert tour of all time, and sold the most concert tickets in one tour ever for his 2017–2019 Divide tour.*

It's easy to look at him now, with the lights, the glitz, and the glam, and assume that his confidence makes sense. But imagine you're a scrawny redheaded kid from Halifax in the United Kingdom who has a lazy eye and a stutter, someone who cries every day before going to school and who later becomes a couch-surfer.

Sheeran shouldn't have had enough confidence to make it happen like that. So our idea of confidence must be wrong. It can't be that confidence is just something we *have*. It must be something we *create*.

And that's good news. Because if Sheeran can create it, so can you.

THE FOUR CONFIDENCE MYTHS

ONE OF THE REASONS I think most of us love Ed Sheeran is that we instinctively recognize him as confident. He's not model-height with the perfect body and perfect hair, and his sound is a bit different from what you usually hear on the radio, so something inside us knows that his success has come about *because* he's confident. I think we're right about that: He has something inside that has made him confident regardless of society's expectations. In fact, he said as much in an inter-

---

* These last two records have since been broken.

view once, where he noted that he had envisioned his future success, knowing that it would likely happen one day.

But, like I mentioned above, he has none of the things that typically would make him that confident. He wasn't born into a superstar family like Miley Cyrus. He doesn't have the classic height and appeal of Glen Powell. And while he's got an angelic voice made for acoustic music, in live shows he uses that *to rap*.

What?

All the confidence, none of the reasons.

Ed Sheeran's story disproves every single thing we think we know about self-confidence. Namely, he dispels the Four Confidence Myths: that confident people are always extroverted, that confident people have no insecurities, that confidence has to be genetic, and that confidence comes only *after* you develop competence.

Confidence ≠ Extroversion

HAVE YOU EVER SEEN former President Barack Obama in an interview?

I've watched plenty of his interviews, and the word "extroverted" has never crossed my mind. In fact, I'd say that he's shy, or even introverted. But he's always attentive, leaning forward, and answering questions, and he seems to be genuine. His confidence totally goes against the first big myth, that confident people are extroverted.

Plus, consider my mom. When she moved from Nicaragua to Canada, she brought a box of books and $100. Within a couple of decades, she'd turned that into a seven-figure language services business. She is perhaps the most confident in-dividual I've ever met, and she's incredibly introverted. She doesn't feel the need to say much, yet her confidence shines out without words.

Truth stands on its own, whereas a lie needs to do a lot of convincing. Similarly, true confidence stands on its own—it doesn't need big talk or lots of words.

Can extroverts be confident? Of course. But one doesn't equal the other. Introverts are often more confident than their extroverted counterparts.

Confidence ≠ Zero Insecurities

WE TEND TO think of confident people as those without inse-curities. But does that fit Sheeran's story—the awkward gin-ger with a stutter and a lazy eye? Not at all.

Is my point that Sheeran isn't confident? No. My point is that he *is* confident, but that he still struggles.

Take a look at Sheeran's story—he did *three hundred* shows just that first year in London. That's a ton of practice on your nerves and your self-confidence. At every show, he was able to confront any fears or doubts right in the face. And after study-ing confident people, I can tell you this: Confident people are full of self-doubt. They just practice dealing with it more, and as a result, they're more confident.

Confident people have more interactions with self-doubt than you think. They just use doubt as a tool to motivate them-selves to overcome challenges.

Confidence ≠ Genetic

MOST OF US view self-confidence as some sort of genetic randomness—we put it in the same category as blue eyes, beautiful legs, or perfect skin. Some were born confident, some weren't. Those who were end up like Sydney Sweeney, starring in rom-coms and hosting *SNL*.

But did Ed Sheeran have any of that?

OK, sure, he has a good voice. But he's fairly short (five feet eight inches, to be exact), doesn't have the classic bad-boy look a lot of people would assume you need to be a pop star, and no one's ever accused him of being an athlete.[8] Then there are the eye, the stutter, and the hair (the hair, of course, is his trademark now).

We think we need to look a certain way or pass a particular threshold of intelligence to be confident. But listen to this story I heard from my team about a guy whose daughter was struggling with a certain disease. The seasoned doctor put it bluntly: "She needs surgery." One of his protégés—who likely wasn't even through residency yet—firmly disagreed.

"I specialize in this *exact* disease; I wrote a two-hundred-page paper on it. There's an alternative treatment that does *not* require surgery."

That's confidence, and that's what we all want. That unwavering feeling based on our experience and expertise, not whatever magical amount of confidence we happen to be born with. We want the innate strength to speak up when we really believe we're right. For some of us, that's in the workplace. Too often, many of us let others put forward bad ideas, or take credit for our good ones. Or we let Carl sneak away with the promotion that we deserved.

Some of us want the boldness to tell our significant other what foods we *really* enjoy. Others want to be able to tell our loved ones, "Thank you for your advice, but no." (Or, as Sheeran said about the "experts" who told him they knew better, we want to learn to "not necessarily listen to what people ha[ve] to say; take it in, sure, but [not as] gospel.")[9]

Maybe we want the confidence to start that company or go back to school. Maybe we're hoping that at our age it's not too late to get back into the dating game, or that at our age it's not too early to get into the investing game.

Regardless, we want the kind of confidence that isn't dependent on society's current version of being genetically gifted or qualified. We want the kind of self-surety that our skin, our body, our age, our abilities are enough, and then we want the boldness to move forward with no other belief but our own. That level of confidence is not something we're born with; it is something we must intentionally learn.

Confidence ≠ Competence

PERHAPS THE BIGGEST of all the myths is this one: that confidence comes *after* competence. We think that if we were better at our job, we'd be more confident in our work. If we could sing better, we'd be more confident at the karaoke bar. If we were a better writer, we'd have more confidence in our writing. With more experience as a parent, we'd be better parents; with more skill in investing, we'd invest more; et cetera.

To be sure, some amount of confidence does come from competence—but there's an obvious problem here: If we move through life believing that competence must *always* come before confidence, then we'll be eternally waiting for that confidence to magically appear before we act. In fact, your life likely proves this wrong. If confidence were dependent on competence, you'd never have learned to walk or read or become an accountant or a dentist or a model or whatever it is that you do. We simply can't wait until we're experts to have the confidence to try something new.

Science has a lot to say about the relationship between competence and confidence. Leadership researcher George P. Hollenbeck and business professor Douglas T. Hall teamed up and wrote an in-depth scientific paper on confidence in the workplace. The most insightful part comes at the end, when they concluded: "The most important part of our message is that self-confidence can be developed. It can be grown through some straightforward, small steps."[10]

Did you catch the key word "developed"? They didn't say that confidence is only for superheroes, certain genetically gifted people, or the lucky few. Instead, they said confidence can be *created*.

Before I started discovering more about confidence, I assumed that the confidence I was born with was the confidence I would always have. But through a process of transformation that began when I looked in the mirror when I was seventy-five pounds overweight, I discovered that *confidence is not an innate character trait. Confidence is a skill set.* And, as with any skill set, you have to practice it. I've seen that truth in others as well.

A coaching client of mine, Caitlin, shows the relationship between confidence and competence absolutely beautifully. She's a basketball player at university. Not a star, but a good player. For as long as she could remember, she was hard on herself—every time she made a mistake in basketball, or even with relationships, she'd beat herself up:

- "Caitlin, you're so stupid."
- "Caitlin, why did you miss that pass?"
- "Of course we lost—look at how many shots
  I missed."

Now, Caitlin wasn't at the time a very positive person. In that sense, one could say she wasn't "competent" at good self-talk. If she had waited for that competency to develop, she'd still be speaking negativity toward herself and her team. Rather, Caitlin made a change and decided to take charge of the way she spoke. She stopped beating herself up and started reframing everything differently. Instead of "I can't believe I missed that pass," she'd say, "Now I know what to work on!" When her team fell behind during a game, she swapped "Another loss, not surprised!" for "We're only two shots away from taking the lead!"

Caitlin consciously *decided* to become better at speaking positively. It felt unnatural to her at first, but over time, as a result of her decisions, she became better and better at positivity. Today, you'd say she's *confident* in her abilities as a positive, upbeat encourager.

We can see, from Caitlin and from science, that competence doesn't always come before confidence. Rather, you can actively decide to do things differently, and confidence can come as a result. Hollenbeck and Hall said it like this:

People take a small risk and make a step toward some important goal . . . succeed in that, and become more confident in their abilities. As a result, they set higher goals, and with success gain more self-confidence, leading to a higher level of aspiration, and so on, and so on. . . . Thus, the overall picture is one of self-confidence as a quality over which the person can have considerable control.[11]

Did you catch that? You have *control* over your confidence.

THE CONFIDENCE NOUN

THE FOUR CONFIDENCE Myths are just the level-one fighters before you get to the "Final Boss." So, are you ready for the Big Villain, the thing we have to call out, name, and destroy early on, as quickly as possible?

It's the Confidence noun.

You probably heard something like this in English class: "A noun is a person, place, thing, or sometimes an idea."

In some technical sense, the word "confidence" is a noun. But the concept most of us have leads us to think it's a thing that we can have or a place at which we arrive.

In reality, confidence is a practice. It's not a place we *get* to; it's a movement, a *doing* of something. When we envision those with extreme amounts of confidence—the CEO who always knows what to say, the yoga instructor who is calm and collected in every situation—we chalk it up to their physique, their knowledge, or their pedigree. But perhaps they've consistently learned to practice showing up. Maybe they've learned that confidence isn't a noun.

Confidence is a verb.

The editors told me not to repeat stuff, but I really, *really* want you to get this. In my work I've spent time with thousands of young, old, and in-between-aged people, people who wanted the confidence to change their relationship, their career, or their parenting style, or just to learn how to speak up more with their friends. And what I've learned is this: Most of us believe that confidence is a genetic gift to some people, but *that's bogus.*

Confidence is a practice, one that you can *choose* to participate in. It isn't just wishful thinking. There's actually a method that works (which we'll get to in the next chapter), but—and this is key—*it's work.* If you were hoping for a couple of magic rocks that would turn you into a confidence aficionado, you picked up the wrong book.

What you'll see in Ed Sheeran's life is a pattern. He experienced nervousness, fear, stage fright, rejection, or disappointment, all of which are normal in the music industry. His response was always simple: *Take another step.* He didn't wait for success to reward him. He decided that he would go first. When Sheeran acted despite the nerves, feeling the fear and stepping through it, he unlocked something so many of us strive to create in our lives—real confidence.

So that brings us to our definition of confidence: to boldly, optimistically *practice* belief in your *abilities* and your *intrinsic worth.*

THAT'S A RAP

YOU DON'T HAVE to wait for anyone or anything to become more confident. I was overweight and I chose confidence. My mom chose to be confident even when her bank account didn't reflect that. Ed Sheeran chose confidence every time he walked onto a bar stage in front of just a few people. Here's what that means for all of us:

- People can practice confidence before they feel physically ready.
- You can practice confidence even with credit card debt.
- Employees unhappy in jobs can practice confidence even if they don't know their next move.
- Teachers can practice confidence even if their students aren't respecting them.
- You can be confident in relationships before your friend or partner has declared their commitment to you.

That's the kind of result I want for every person reading this—I want the coffee shop you wish to open, your desire to get in better shape, your hope to be a better parent, or your dream of being the CEO of your own company to become a reality. To create the future you want by starting with your own beliefs about your abilities and worth. Or, in a word, *confidence.* That confidence becomes the difference between never getting started and making the first move toward your goal. Confidence is what allows you to take an early withdrawal on your future success—"I'm already taking steps toward what I want"—before others even comment on it. With confidence you can push past the voices, move beyond the points of failure, and live without regret. You don't need external validation. You can *feel* confident and *believe* in yourself, even without society's stamp of acceptance. Trust me, it's a way better way to live.

You could live your whole life allowing your confidence to be swayed by others' opinions and your success to be determined by circumstance, *or* you could start today, moving toward the life that you want; in the absolute worst-case scenario you make moves toward your desired goals and feel better along the way. What do you think?

"Of course, Juan, I want the self-confidence route. That's why I'm reading this!"

Well, great. We're on the right page at exactly the right time.

In the next chapter, we're going to break down confidence in a step-by-step way that *anyone can start using.* If you look around, you'll find fitness methods that work, approaches that can help your newborn baby sleep better, business plans that help you succeed, and educational programs that get you a degree; all of them utilize a step-by-step approach. Now you'll learn a science-backed method to help you achieve confidence that works the exact same way: Follow the steps and you'll have more confidence.

This isn't going to be a quick fix; building confidence is a lifelong endeavor. But if you're prepared to put in the work, the book you're holding can revolutionize your life and show you just how great your relationships and life can be.

It's important to remember that I'm an action guy. The information here must be not only retained but practiced as well. So I'll try to make this book an easy go-to reference for your confidence. At the end of every chapter I'll offer a recap and a call to action. Using the recap, you'll be able to quickly remember the biggest takeaways from the chapter and come back later to refresh your memory.

Confidence Cheat Sheet

- Most of us recognize the type of confidence we want, but then misunderstand how we gain it. We want the sort of confidence that Ed Sheeran seems to have, but then we forget that he doesn't have the usual factors most of us associate with confidence—the height, the extroversion, the suave persona.
- Our definition of confidence: to boldly, optimistically *practice* belief in your *abilities* and your *intrinsic worth.*
- Science has shown that confidence is not an inherited trait; rather, it can be developed by anyone.
- Debunking the Four Confidence Myths:

  - **Confidence ≠ extroversion**
  - **Confidence ≠ zero insecurities**
  - **Confidence ≠ genetic**
  - **Confidence ≠ competence**

- It's time to get to work creating confidence!

Micro-Step

Every chapter, we're going to end with an action item.

For this chapter, it's easy! Write down the specific actions you'd like to take as a result of reading this book and becoming more confident.

2.

One Ounce at a Time

———

The great victory, which appears so simple today,
was the result of a series of
small victories that went unnoticed.

—PAULO COELHO

N 1970, IN THE BEAUTIFUL TOWN OF EUGENE, OREGON, BILL Bowerman was having breakfast with his family. The family was making waffles and all seemed peaceful. No one knew that this moment would become the story the world tells about how Bowerman reinvented shoes and catapulted a small company into one of the most recognized brands in the world.

I imagine things were going as usual—"Honey, can you pass the butter?" "Yes, dear. Would you like another glass of orange juice?"—but somewhere between sips of orange juice and bites of waffle, a lightning bolt hit Bowerman. He was a track coach at the University of Oregon, where the university had just put in a new type of running surface, and Bowerman was hoping for a shoe that could grip the surface without using cleats or spikes. That's when he spotted the pattern on the waffle iron.

After (allegedly) getting permission from his wife to use what had been a wedding present to satisfy his insatiable appetite for improved footwear, he took the waffle iron out to the garage and started dumping polyurethane onto the plates. The result was a surface that had enough grooves to reliably grip many surfaces. The waffle iron was ruined, but footwear was reinvented.

Bowerman sent a friend this new design (attached to the bottom of a running shoe), and eventually the two of them launched the creation at Blue Ribbon Sports, calling the shoe the Cortez. That shoe is *still* in production at their company, whose name they'd later change to Nike, named after the Greek goddess of victory.[1]

Not only had Bowerman created one of the bestselling shoes of all time, but he'd launched modern athletic footwear and turned an unknown running-shoe company into one of the most recognized brands in the world. By 2022, Nike was worth $240 billion.[2] Not bad for a waffle iron.

———

THAT WAFFLE IRON moment is pure magic for storytellers and journalists. How do you beat an aha moment that starts with a breakfast-making appliance? But the truth is more complex—Bowerman didn't just suddenly have a good idea. He was a running coach who for decades had been obsessed with what goes on the bottom of a track star's feet. Over the course of his long career as head coach at the University of Oregon, he'd eventually help coach:

- Twenty-two world record holders
- Twenty-four NCAA title holders

- Thirty-three Olympians
- Sixty-four All-Americans

And by the time he was pouring syrup on his waffles in 1970, he had been tinkering for years with his athletes' shoes, breaking them down, tweaking them, and passing along his new concoction to a collegiate runner. He'd watch their performance, and then he'd start all over again, moving a piece of fabric this way, tugging a strap that way, deconstructing the sole, on and on, constant small improvements. Here's how Phil Knight, co-founder of Nike, who was also coached by Bowerman, said it in his memoir, *Shoe Dog:*

> He was obsessed with how human beings are shod. In the four years I'd run for him at Oregon, Bowerman was constantly sneaking into our lockers and stealing our footwear. He'd spend days tearing them apart, stitching them back up, then hand them back with some minor modification, which made us either run like deer or bleed. Regardless of the results, he never stopped. He was determined to find new ways of bolstering the instep, cushioning the midsole, building out more room for the forefoot.[3] He always had some new design, some new scheme to make our shoes sleeker, softer, lighter. Especially lighter. One ounce sliced off a pair of shoes, he said, is equivalent to 55 pounds over one mile.[4]

And that's how lasting success is usually developed—not by a stroke of waffle lightning but by the slow drip of microshifts over time. The multibillion-dollar company that we all can recognize from a single swoosh was built on thousands of small moments of a guy staring at shoes and pushing for just one more ounce of positive change.

It happens that way for all of us—one small ounce of change, compounded over time, creates a world of difference. Let's say you are filled with self-doubt every day when you wake up. What if you simply told yourself just before your feet hit the ground, "Today's going to be a good day"? Imagine how different your life would be in a few months without changing anything else.

Let's say that you're not confident speaking up in your friend group, and you always default to agreeing with the consensus. You could make it a goal to say something you *really* believe in once in every hangout, even if you think someone will laugh at you. You don't have to start with religion and politics; you could start by saying that you really *don't* like Chinese food. Assuming you hang out with friends about once a week, by the end of the year you'd have fifty chances to practice saying what you believe. Can you imagine how much more confident you'd be with that simple change after just one year?

If you're an entrepreneur who feels terrible about charging too much, why not just raise your current price by a few dollars? Then, next time, do it again.

In each of those scenarios, doing the small thing repeatedly will, *at the very least,* give you more confidence to do those small things again the next time.

But it's more likely that those small steps will open the door for bigger moments, for aha moments like the one in the waffle iron story.

One ounce of improvement isn't much, but when you keep

at it, it compounds, and over time that creates the necessary runway for bigger successes.

BJ FOGG'S ONE LITTLE TOOTH

SO I DIDN'T get that "tell yourself it's going to be a good day" idea from my own mind. It came from author BJ Fogg, writer of the smash hit *Tiny Habits*.

Fogg is a behavioral scientist, and in his book he tackles one particular task dentists, mothers, and lovers have been attempting to push people toward for decades: flossing.

The majority of people know flossing is healthy for them, but it's not ingrained into their daily routine like brushing their teeth. Fogg wanted to know why. So he attempted to become a "flosser" himself. The trouble was, flossing was too much work. He tried all sorts of things to stick with it, but nothing worked—until an idea hit him. He would try breaking down his goal of flossing every night into something even smaller: flossing only one tooth.

How simple is that? Anyone can make themselves floss just *one* tooth. Sure, if you've never flossed, it still requires you to step outside your comfort zone. But hey, it's one tooth. Anyone can do that, right? So Fogg flossed one tooth the first night, then discarded the floss. The next night, he did the same.

After a while, he felt pretty confident in his ability to floss just one tooth. And guess what? You know how easy it is, once you've gotten over the initial hurdle of pulling out the floss and applying it to your teeth, to go ahead and floss just one *more* tooth?

The same is true for building your confidence. Big confidence starts with small but meaningful steps toward a larger goal.

Maybe you want to be a public speaker, write a book, get a promotion, start a company, or have a thriving friend group where you can be your authentic self. *All* great confidence goals. But guess what? They're probably too big to tackle *today*.

Instead, set the goal and define a meaningful step, a teeny-tiny, one-tooth-at-a-time step. An action that requires courage, but only a small amount of it. Actions that, once initiated, build confidence by default ("Look what I did!") and eventually start to shift your identity into someone new. Whatever your confidence goal is—be able to ask out the guy at the gym, rapidly change your career, conquer your social anxiety, speak in front of a crowd of at least a thousand—the key to getting there is by starting microscopically small.

If you have severe social anxiety, try just putting one coffee date on the calendar. Just *one*. Text the person who is most likely to say yes, pick somewhere that's emotionally and logistically easy to get to, spend half an hour with them, then *check, please!* You've already taken courageous action. Now the next time you get scared about going out in public, you can remind yourself, "Look what I did," which affords proof that you did that one small thing. You "flossed one tooth," and it wasn't so hard.

Confidence is a muscle, and it has to be exercised. We all have a different "natural starting speed" when it comes to our confidence journey, and the goal isn't to race anyone else. It's to improve. When Bowerman coached his track runners, clearly they all had different starting speeds and endurance capabilities. He didn't judge the success of his shoe-tinkering by whether or not an athlete won a race against others; rather,

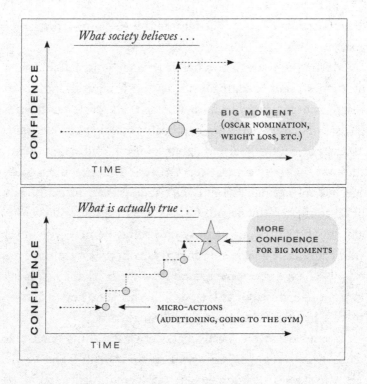

his criterion was whether or not a micro-shift *improved that runner's ability.*

So don't compare yourself to anyone else. Rather, look at whether or not a small step improves *your* confidence.

ONE SMALL STEP TO A
BIGGER PATTERN OF CHANGE

BOWERMAN FOLLOWED A pattern to his success—and it's the same one Sheeran and Fogg followed as well. Each of their stories follows exactly the same, simple arc.

First, each had goals, dreams, and desires that *excited* each of them individually.

That excitement led to them having *enough courage* to do some hard things. Bowerman had to keep tearing down and rebuilding shoes (plus he had to be brave enough to ask his wife to destroy their kitchen appliance). Sheeran was stoked enough about music that he was willing to sleep on London Underground trains—"the tube"—between gigs, time after time. The connection between excitement and courage really matters, because if you're going to get through some inevitable discomfort, you need to have something worth fighting for.

Next, each of them started with a small step toward a larger goal—Sheeran did small gigs for charities, Bowerman reformulated pieces of shoes, and Fogg flossed one tooth. Atomically small stuff, really.

Finally, they'd find evidence after they'd taken action. And that evidence wasn't always *success*—Sheeran didn't get offered a music deal after one gig, and Fogg didn't fix his flossing problem after getting one tooth flossed. However, each of their actions proved something: Trying didn't kill them, and they'd proven to themselves that *at least they tried*. That attempt fueled their next attempt, and the next, and the next.

For the shoe god Bowerman, it looked like this: obsession with shoes → courageous enough to tear down a shoe → shaved off one ounce of weight → evidence of one attempt.

For Sheeran, his pattern looked very, very similar: excited to be in music → bold enough to face rejection → did a small gig → felt better about trying a bigger one.

For Fogg: desire to have better dental hygiene → brave enough to admit he wasn't good at flossing all his teeth (yet) → flossed one tooth → one tooth-flossing closer to a better smile.

Now, here's where it gets crazy. What do you think happens to the shoe-obsessed Bowerman after he shaves off *one ounce* of weight? What do you think happens to Sheeran after *one person* asks him to sign an autograph? Or how about Fogg—what do you think happens to him after he celebrates *having one tooth* flossed? They get excited *all over again,* and start the cycle again: excitement for the change, courage to face the problem, small action, proof that it works . . . all building more excitement for the next go-round.

Now, what if we could take that same cycle and apply it to our confidence? What if we could build confidence in the same step-by-step way that Bowerman built his better shoes, Sheeran found his musical prowess, and Fogg obtained his flossing routine? It turns out that's *exactly* how you build confidence.

I first discovered this when I was reviewing how I'd gone from the overweight Nicaraguan kid who was pretending to be something I wasn't to being the guy onstage speaking at a conference with thousands of attendees. I had to ask myself how *that* kid only a decade later had changed his entire self-image. For me, it started with someone (a good friend, Luis) showing me a better life, getting me *excited* about what mine could look like. From there, I decided I'd start facing some of my life problems—and I had a lot to choose from at the time, from relationship problems to weight problems. One area I really zoomed in on was my career goals. For that, I took baby steps into the career I wanted, one that I hadn't even remotely begun (public speaking). At first I just made it a goal to email ten potential clients a week to offer my "services."

The first week, all ten declined. Well, actually, most of them declined to even decline. They just ignored me. But you know what? I had proof that I could send an email. So I tried it again. And again. Eventually, someone did ask me to come speak . . . to senior citizens at a restaurant. I counted it as a win!

Based on this small win, I had a little more energy and courage to email more clients, so I did, which eventually brought about another win—this one just a tad bigger. All along the way, not only was my career growing, but, far more importantly, my confidence was, too.

THE CONFIDENCE CYCLE

IN THE LAST CHAPTER, I told you about Hollenbeck and Hall, who researched self-confidence, ultimately determining that you can develop it. But you know what else they determined? *That the path to self-confidence is a self-reinforcing cycle.*

I'd already picked up on this well before I read the Hollenbeck and Hall study, but it is reassuring to know that my experience, my teachings, and my observations of others are backed up by science.

After giving speech after speech on this cycle, seeing it grow confidence in myself and others, and refining it meticulously over the last few years, here, in a nutshell is how I now explain the Confidence Cycle:

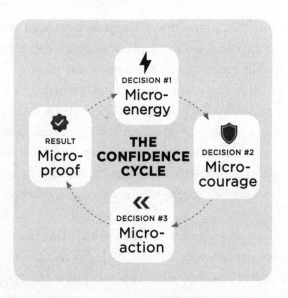

- **MICRO-ENERGY.** Direct excitement toward the area of improvement.
- **MICRO-COURAGE.** Find the bravery to move through discomfort.
- **MICRO-ACTION.** Complete a small action.
- **MICRO-PROOF.** Receive evidence that you are headed in the right direction, which gives you more confidence, thus continuing the cycle.

Importantly, you can use this cycle, right now, to build confidence in just one area, or in your life as a whole.

Let's take Alex, who works from home. She just got a new job in marketing and is adapting to her team and her new schedule. She lives in a major city, which seems like it would be a hot spot for meeting new people, but remote work has made it hard for her to make friends. After the pandemic, her social skills haven't been the same.

For Alex, building a loving community was always a dream. Only problem? Over the past few years, she has developed social anxiety. It all started by feeling nervous about speaking up at work, and then it graduated into her refusing to go into social situations where she didn't know everyone.

She wanted to change her confidence, particularly in relationships. Honestly, she wanted to become a social butterfly, but she just didn't know how. So she decided on a micro-step, a super-tiny one: "What if I start by getting comfortable being around new people?"

Then she broke it down into something very concrete, ultimately deciding she'd take her at-home work to the local coffee shop, where she'd at least be around new people. Think of how energizing and relieving this was—that she didn't have to suddenly become a cheerleader personality who was Miss Popular. Instead, she could relax, go to a coffee shop (which probably had drinks she enjoyed, at the very least), and get comfortable.

After several days of doing this, she grew accustomed to seeing the same faces day in and day out, and her next confidence move came almost by accident. After nine visits to the same coffee shop, Alex surprised herself when she heard these words fly from her mouth: "I love your shirt! Where did you get it?" She was totally in disbelief that she, the social anxiety queen, had sparked a conversation with a total stranger.

And guess what? No one called her crazy. In fact, she was rewarded for it.

Stranger: "Thanks so much! I actually got it from a local shop down the street. Want me to send you the link?"

Just like that, they exchanged numbers, started meeting up at that same coffee shop, and even planned a dinner a few weeks later. Fast-forward to a few months later . . . and Alex now says hi to people at the coffee shop, at the gym, on work trips, and in other places. What started as a simple hello compounded. Does Alex still get nervous? Of course. Does she do it anyway? Absolutely. Why? Because she started the cycle, and her confidence will never be the same again.

Alex's Confidence Cycle looked like this:

- **MICRO-ENERGY.** Alex broke down her confidence goal into something so small—work at a coffee shop—she immediately felt relief and excitement about her confidence goals.
- **MICRO-COURAGE.** She only needed enough courage to show up at the coffee shop.
- **MICRO-ACTION.** She went to the same coffee shop for over two weeks.
- **MICRO-PROOF.** She got a triple-dip on proof: She showed up at a place full of strangers (showing herself that she wasn't as anxious as she thought), she complimented a stranger without thinking about it (surprising herself with her own confidence), and then she and the stranger became friends.

Another example is Randall, who had always dreamed of working at Disney. Somehow he'd struggled through an audition and was asked to perform as Anakin Skywalker (a real dream for any *Star Wars* nerd).

But a couple of days into training, it wasn't going well. He was thrust right into the middle of arguably one of their toughest programs (*Star Wars Weekends*) with the most seasoned performers at the company and the toughest acting coaches. Everything was eight notches over his head, and everyone else had years of experience and lots of dance training. Then there was Randall, who was asking, "Where do I stand, exactly?"

Randall clearly had no experience (and it was showing). Whatever confidence he had at the beginning was totally shattered toward the end of his training, when his coaches sent him home with a whole *list* of notes. "We'll stop at ten big notes," they'd said. Staring at his notes, Randall was ready to toss in the light saber.

Just before he called it quits, he asked a fellow performer for advice. She looked at his journal of notes and her eyes got big. "That is a ton of notes," she remarked.

But then she said something that changed everything.

"Randall, why not try this? Just focus *on one thing*. Here, put your shoulders back and walk across the room with your chest out."

OK, that's silly, but easy, he thought.

Randall walked across the room.

"You look awesome, Randall!"

His confidence immediately swelled.

"Instead of focusing on these notes," she said, literally tossing the notebook aside, "simply practice walking like you just did. Forget everything else they said."

So Randall did. He *walked*. He didn't run lines. He didn't learn to dance better, speak more clearly, or wield a light saber. He just walked. He even had his friends film him while he walked. Eventually his walking got so good that one of his friends who was filming him *got scared of him* as he walked up!

- **MICRO-ENERGY.** His friend persuaded him to put aside the notes, and then she gave him something simple he could do.
- **MICRO-COURAGE.** Randall only needed enough courage to walk.
- **MICRO-ACTION.** He (quite literally) just took a small step.
- **MICRO-PROOF.** Every time he walked, he felt a little better about his stage presence . . . until one day his friend got scared of him because of how he walked!

Within a few months, Randall's confidence had grown so much as a performer, guests were writing letters to Walt Disney World management about how incredible he was. Within a couple of years, he was training others in his department. Within a decade, he was performing on Broadway-level stages.

That's the power of building confidence one step at a time and allowing that step to build a pattern of ever-increasing confidence.

———

REMEMBER, THIS WHOLE thing is a cycle, and I find that it *best starts with energy*. For now, I've given you the super-simple version of the Confidence Cycle, so you can get going immediately on building confidence anywhere in your life. I wholeheartedly stand by this simplicity.

However, there are a ton of ways you can carry out each of the Confidence Cycle steps, particularly the micro-energy piece. We'll talk about the other methods of creating energy and excitement as the book goes on—like energy anchors—

but for now, know that once you've broken your big goals down into something small, you'll feel immediate relief and excitement!

Also, a quick note about proof. We'll go over this later, but I already know the pushback your mind is giving you: *What if I take courageous action on something, and my only "proof" is that I failed? What then, Juan? What then?*

I totally get that. But "proof" doesn't mean you succeeded. It means you completed the cycle. Even if your worst fears came true, you have the proof that you're still standing, and that you had the courage to take a small step *even though* it failed. In a way, failure has the opportunity to give you even more confidence than success does. Psychologist Albert Bandura put it like this: "It is not the sheer intensity of emotional and physical reactions that is important but rather how they are *perceived* and *interpreted*."[5]

In other words, even if the stranger whose shirt Alex complimented had looked at her and then run off without replying, Alex would still have had proof that she'd done it—and right there, already, her perception of herself (dare I say her confidence?) could evolve, just because she took a small step. In fact, even if Alex hadn't said anything to anyone for six months at that coffee shop, guess what? She still would have had proof that at least she'd gotten out of her home. Whenever you take action, the evidence, in the worst-case scenario, is that you made an attempt you hadn't made before. And that's evidence enough to start the cycle again!

I knew a guy (note to readers: It was me) whose lovely wife had the brilliant idea to bring him along to her beloved SoulCycle class. Keep in mind that this guy had never set foot in a SoulCycle class before, or even any spin class. If you, too, are unfamiliar with that class, here's a snapshot: You're in a completely dark room with lit candles all around, and the music is blaring. You strap your feet into a spin bike, grab your towel, and face a wall-sized mirror behind the instructor. Oh, and everyone is wearing what feel like tap dancing shoes. This guy happened to be the only male in the room. As everyone began to move to the music, somehow perfectly performing an unspoken choreography, the five-foot instructor with Rapunzel-style hair down to her knees introduced herself: "Hi, everyone! Are you ready to step into the grace you deserve and experience the gratitude and abundance of the day?"

The resounding "Wooo!" vibrated the mirror on the wall.

Meanwhile, this guy was still trying to clip in his right foot without falling over.

Between trying to keep up with the choreography, dealing with the towels flicking all over the place, and wheezing out responses to the instructor's questions, he felt completely out of sync. For the entirety of that forty-five-minute class, he was drenched in sweat, utterly confused, and convinced that he was the least competent person in the room (which was probably true).

But you know what? This guy didn't let it destroy his confidence. Instead, he went with it, laughing it off as (yet another) of his insanely goofy ideas—this time, the notion that he could keep up with his amazing wife. Even with his lack of competence, which could have been viewed as evidence that he had no idea what he was doing, he focused on the fact that he finished the class.

Here are a few ways your failures can act as proof to restart the Confidence Cycle:

Say you always wanted to be a fashion blogger, but you aren't confident that you're even a good writer. Nevertheless, you start by putting up a listicle—"12 Things to Wear in the Fall." Only your mom reads it. Guess what? *You now have proof that you can publish a blog online.*

Maybe you aren't confident about the way you look in pictures. So you commit to taking a selfie once a week and posting it online. Sure enough, you don't like your angles, and you think that outfit isn't doing you any favors. Guess what? *You posted it anyway.*

Perhaps you aren't confident that you're good enough to get the work promotion you've wanted for nearly a decade. But this time you apply for it and get interviewed . . . and sure enough, they go with someone else. Guess what? *You now know how easy it is to apply.* (Plus, you got some face time in with the people who you hope will be hiring you next time around.)

Maybe you want to get in better shape, but you're totally sure that at the gym you're going to look like an idiot on the complicated machines. So you show up, and sure enough, you use one of them wrong. A gymhead comes by and tells you the right way. *Well, now you can be confident that next time you'll know how to use at least one of them.*

On and on . . . as long as you perceive the "failure" correctly, every actionable step toward your confidence goals is proof that will give you enough energy to restart the cycle.

DEFINE YOUR GOLDILOCKS STEP

PSYCHOLOGIST AND HARVARD Business School professor emerita Teresa M. Amabile and researcher Steven J. Kramer dove deep into what makes teams productive and creative at work. They analyzed thousands of journal entries written by hundreds of employees, and they boiled down their findings to some remarkably simple takeaways. Essentially, they found that teams that seemed the happiest and most productive were those that made simple, small moves toward meaningful, purposeful work. Here's an insightful passage from an article they published in the *Harvard Business Review:*

> Of all the things that can boost emotions, motivation, and perceptions during a workday, the single most important is *making progress* in meaningful work. And the more *frequently* people experience that sense of progress, the more likely they are to be creatively productive in the long run. Whether they are trying to solve a major scientific mystery or simply produce a high-quality product or service, everyday progress—*even a small win*—can make all the difference in how they feel and perform.[6]

Other studies, like one by Daniel Chambliss that followed the progress of elite swimmers, have showed similar results: What matters is repeated progress toward something meaningful.[7] You already know that building your confidence is meaningful; that's why you're reading this book! Now, you just need to ensure you're constantly making *small steps* to get there. So, how small should you make that next small step?

Based on tons of research, the goal is to make your next confidence step small enough that you can accomplish it, but big enough that it's actually moving you toward where you want to go. So, not too big, not too small, just right. I call it the Goldilocks step.

Here's how it breaks down:

1. Focus on one area of your life you want to have more confidence in.
2. Define a small step toward progress that feels somewhat uncomfortable but not impossible.
3. Do the small step!
4. Celebrate the win.
5. Repeat, iterating on how small your step was—you want to keep making progress.

The step should be a slight stretch, but not something that pushes you so hard that you snap, nor that goes so easy that there's no tension. You should feel tension in your small step, but it should be achievable. Here's how a few people I know have put the Goldilocks step into practice:

Beth wanted to be a public speaker. She identified that in order to get confident in public speaking, she needed to find opportunities to be in front of an audience. Her step was that simple—she didn't need to be in a stadium, get paid, or be a keynote headliner. She needed simply to be in front of audiences. That could be doing a reading at church, volunteering to give a talk at a local library, or going to a senior center and delivering a speech. Any of those was, for her, a Goldilocks step: big enough to be progress, but small enough to be possible.

Aaron wanted to find a life partner. So, he defined his small step as going on a date, which he wasn't really doing much of at the time. He went on a date, then another, then another. While the goal was meaningful—find a long-term romantic partner—he didn't need to jump into that right away. When he examined his life, it was easy to see that he wasn't even dating regularly, so that became his small step.

Mike was someone who wanted to get better at managing his finances, and he knew it was going to take facing the fear of looking at his financial situation. Feeling discouraged by how daunting it seemed, he created a small step: spend twenty minutes every week focusing on his investments. The progress he was making every week motivated him to keep going.

Though it may seem simple, what Beth, Aaron, and Mike did was extraordinary. They defined a small step, then executed on it, and in doing so set the course to change their confidence. Every time they completed a step—by speaking in front of an audience, going on a date, or reviewing their finances—they had more confidence for the next time. Over time, as those small steps became second nature, they gained confidence to take bigger ones.

What's the current area you're struggling in? If you're a manager who wishes she had more confidence with her employees because you feel like you "never speak up" when they need constructive criticism, you could define your Goldilocks step as "giving them one piece of feedback every week."

If you're not confident about your professional writing, you could commit to posting once every week on your LinkedIn.

If you're struggling with your confidence at making friends, make a commitment to set up one coffee hangout every two weeks with one friend.

Over time, you can iterate on these goals. If they're too hard, back it up. If they're too easy or if after doing them you feel like you didn't accomplish enough, increase the goal slightly. In my experience, most people start too big, just like Fogg's experiments with flossing—no matter how simple and easy something seems, you usually need to make the task easier.

One last note, about *celebration*.

Importantly, baby steps forward create lasting change because they're noticed *and celebrated*. In Fogg's work, he explicitly said as much, noting that celebration was a key factor in building his habit. Fogg didn't wait to celebrate until his dentist told him he had no cavities; he did a little dance *every time* he flossed one tooth. Each time he celebrated these tiny steps, his brain was more likely to complete that action the next day, because there was positive emotion tied to the action. (We'll talk more about creating this type of energy later.)

DON'T DESPISE SMALL BEGINNINGS

THERE'S AN ANCIENT proverb that says, "Do not despise these small beginnings." The Confidence Cycle is designed to be small, really small. I'm not trying to get you to run a marathon of confidence. I'm trying to get you to take *just one step out the door.*

And that's what you should have received in this chapter—a boiled-down, overly simplistic, you-haven't-even-read-the-book-yet way to put the Confidence Cycle into action in your own life. Create *micro-energy* by focusing on one small action you can take; find some *micro-courage* to take that small step; do the *micro-action;* find the *micro-proof* that, no matter what, you did the thing. Then enjoy your evolved identity with more confidence for the next go-round.

Don't worry; throughout our time together, I'll give you far more specific tactics and strategies to increase your confidence. But that's the Confidence Cycle in a nutshell.

Confidence Cheat Sheet

- One-ounce shifts have the power to change your life in a big way. *If you want to achieve big, think small.*
- The Confidence Cycle:

1. **MICRO-ENERGY.** Direct new (or renewed) excitement toward the area of improvement.
2. **MICRO-COURAGE.** Find the bravery to move through discomfort.
3. **MICRO-ACTION.** Complete a small action.
4. **MICRO-PROOF.** Receive evidence that you are headed in the right direction, which gives you more confidence, thus continuing the cycle.

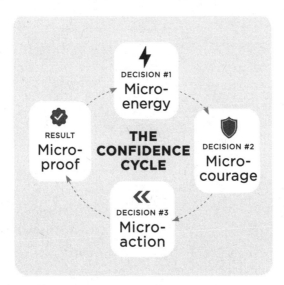

Micro-Step

For big confidence, we need to start small. It is never the big win that defines who we are; it is always the daily micro-steps we take toward our desired future.

Think about what areas of life you'd like to apply the Confidence Cycle to. It can be relationships, finances, career, or even improving your mindset. Having clarity on what you want to improve will help you design the road map to create your desired life.

Micro-Energy

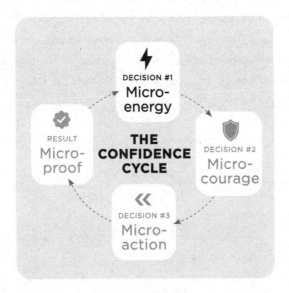

CONFIDENCE CYCLE ENERGY: *A spark of anticipation that gets you excited enough to face something uncomfortable.*

So many of us get deterred from our pursuit of confidence because we rely on sheer willpower to motivate us. *Next time, I'll speak up. I'll try to be more candid with my spouse. I'll do my best to make more eye contact.*

But willpower can't be the starting place. It's too short-lived.

In the next two chapters, we'll argue that the courage you need to move through the Confidence Cycle is actually the *byproduct of energy*—an excitement that you feel when your life is made up of things you enjoy (and devoid of things you hate).

To build a more confident *you,* you need to start by infusing more energy into your life and directing it toward your goals. Then you'll have the courage to take the action necessary (like speak up at the meeting or tell your kids no). From there, you'll be moving around the Confidence Cycle.

3.

The Five Micro-Energy Boosters

---

*People meet your energy before
they meet you.*

—JUAN BENDAÑA

HAVE A FRIEND, DEE, WHO'S BEEN AN ALMOST DELUSIONAL optimist since she was six years old. In the midst of her parents' economic struggles, she told herself, *One day, I'm going to buy my mom and dad a big, fancy house.* In the meantime, her mom was a janitor, and her dad worked multiple jobs. But none of that hardship seemed to faze Dee.

When Dee became an adult, her work didn't afford her enough money to fulfill her dream of buying her parents a home. Still, Dee's delusional optimism prevailed. Then one day she got her shot—she applied for a TV show, *Survivor*, and was somehow selected. From the moment she found out she'd be on the show, she had a sense of excitement.

"I'm going to win the $1 million," she told her brother before she boarded the plane to Fiji. Then she looked over at her parents: "Don't worry about me. Next time you see me, I'll be a millionaire."

I hesitate to tell you the rest of the story, (a) because you'll think I'm lying and (b) because you'll think that I'm trying to pitch you the Law of Attraction or a version of "name it and claim it." Because, to everyone's surprise, Dee *did* win the money. She used it, of course, to take care of her parents.

The point isn't that she ended up winning the money, because there's a big chance she might not have. However, by the time Dee was selected to be on *Survivor,* she'd already started a small but successful business. Before that, she'd worked as an assistant, and before that, at a pharmacy. Dee was constantly moving forward, pushing upward, and if she'd continued on her path she certainly would have been able to buy her parents a home at some point, even without the *Survivor* money. And *that's* the point.

The anticipation of her future energized her present. It gave her courage to face the economic realities she saw around her. And through it all, she never lost confidence in herself. That's what energy does: It's a little bit of excitement that makes taking the next step in the Confidence Cycle, courage, come a bit easier.

INTRODUCTION TO ENERGY

WHEN I INFORMED my team that the first step in the Confidence Cycle is *energy,* my good man Josh, our resident skeptic, nearly fell out of his chair. Every grand idea has to pass his quality-assurance sniff test, and his standards are high. I looked at his face and I could tell what he was thinking: *"Energy" sounds like some kumbaya hippie nonsense.*

But that's not what I mean by energy. Your goal is to have more confidence, right? (If you thought you were reading a book on how to build a model airplane, I'm really surprised you're still reading.) As we've learned, confidence is a verb, something you do, not a gift. Per our definition, our confidence can be increased or decreased, and it is a *practice.*

Now, this is where a lot of people get it wrong. They just jump in with practice, attempting to create more confidence with courage. But courage is the *second* step in the Confidence Cycle.

People jump into things this way all the time. They try to use courage (often calling it "willpower" or "motivation") for all sorts of personal improvements—to lose weight, to conquer their fears, to overcome addiction, and so on. But willpower is short-lived. It can get you to the starting line a few times, but eventually, courage alone gives out. That's why gyms are full in January and empty by March. It's why Navy SEAL training has a nearly 80 percent attrition rate. It's why people don't finish college. They start with boldness, address little else in their life, and eventually fall flat.

Let's take two people, Ethan and Catherine. They're similar people—in their early thirties, ten years into their career. They've reached points where to move up in their company, they'll need to learn to speak in front of people. The trouble is, they're both *terrified.*

So, both of them sign up for a local group that helps you get comfortable speaking in front of others, with hands-on practice in larger and larger groups. It's a tough four-month program, with two weekly classes plus homework.

Courageous Catherine goes about this boldly. Speech class is on Tuesday and Thursday nights, so she tells her fiancé they'll have to cancel their weekly date night for a while. Every week, she shows up to her classes, no matter what's going on at work. Even when her boss asks her to take on some additional projects and she says yes, she still manages to squeeze in time for her speech class. Every week, even with the extra work, she stays committed—often going straight from work to get to class on time. But every week, she hates going. She's beyond stressed, both at work and at speech class, and her burnout starts spilling into her relationships with her friends and her fiancé.

Energy Ethan also wants a promotion, and he, too, hates public speaking, maybe even more than Catherine does. Being generally less bold than Catherine, he attacks the problem differently. First, he lets his work know that for the next few months, he won't be as available for extra projects because he's committed to his speech class, which in the long run will benefit both his professional career and his workplace. Energy Ethan tells his fiancée that they'll have to cancel their Thursday-night pickleball outings for the time being but asks if she'd be interested in coming to hear him speak that night instead. She agrees. To ensure he finishes his homework (which he hates), he gets up extra early in the morning to do it at his favorite local café, telling himself, *I'll treat myself to that guilty-pleasure drink every time I go.* Then, knowing he's going to now dislike Tuesday and Thursday nights for the next four months (Thursdays most of all, because that's when he'll have to give a weekly speech), he buys bottles of his favorite wine. For every speech he gives, both he and his fiancée will drink a glass or two. With that in mind, he almost looks *forward* to speech night.

So, there's stressed-out, overworked, relationally drained Courageous Catherine, and then there's Energy Ethan. Which one do you think is going to finish speech class? Yeah. I'd put all my money on Energy Ethan.

In *Chef* (one of my favorite movies), an artistic chef is working at a fine-dining restaurant, and he's miserable. He's having to meet the cooking demands of others, and others aren't letting him explore new ideas with dishes. One day he hits a tipping point, quits the restaurant, starts a food truck, and rediscovers his passion for cooking. Was starting a food truck *easy*? No way. It entailed all kinds of work—renovation, financial troubles, hiring and firing employees, and a million other things. It would have been easier to stay inside the soulless kitchen. But he found energy for his food truck (and his life) by focusing on what he wanted—to create inspirational dishes. He didn't find what he wanted by just "sucking it up"; he got his cooking mojo back by adding energy into his life.

In the same way, Courageous Catherine and Energy Ethan have the same fears and were hoping to build confidence in the same area. Much looked the same in both of their lives, but Catherine thought she could do it with willpower, motivation, and courage alone, while Ethan looked at his situation and added elements to make him excited. Notice how he did two things:

1. Proactively consider what would kill his energy (the stress from work, the strain on his relationship, the horror of homework, and the dread of having to speak in front of people)
2. Add in activities that would increase his energy (like the wine-night reward or inviting his fiancée to watch him speak)

So, when I write "energy" I'm not talking about the kind people in Sedona manufacture when they rub two crystals together. I'm talking about the kind of energy that gets you excited about life:

- That feeling you get the day before you go on vacation
- The recharge you get during your favorite weekly activities (whether reading, tennis, drawing, painting, or watching *Suits*)
- The anticipation that grips you as you look forward to a concert, a date night, or an outing with your friends

The sciences use the term "activation energy." In chemistry, that term "describes the amount of energy needed to initiate the reaction."[1] So, if you want to make a chemical reaction, you need a certain amount of initial energy to start that chain of events.

Psychologists have co-opted this term to mean "the motivation required to begin a task."[2] I love that definition! It describes the mental effort you need to begin, and not just mental "willpower" or "resilience." So, when we apply that to confidence, here's how I define it: *The energy you want is a spark of anticipation that gets you excited enough to face something uncomfortable.*

Importantly, energy sparks don't have to be huge. Think back to Energy Ethan: looking forward to a sip of wine gave him just enough excitement to get to speech class.

When it comes to our confidence, with a little spark of energy you'll be able to start a chain of events that will prove to you that you're someone different from who you thought you were. Energy Ethan was able to go to speech class and become more confident in his public speaking. Dee was able to confidently face her current financial issues because her future vision excited her. Bowerman (the shoe god from earlier) kept running around the track of improvement (see what I did there?) because he was so excited every time he shaved off an ounce of weight from his new shoes.

What do you need to energize *you*?

INTRODUCING THE FIVE
MICRO-ENERGY BOOSTERS

THINK ABOUT THIS: If your week were full of things you loved, would you be more committed to the few things you can't stand? That weekly one-on-one that you hate going to wouldn't be so bad if you got to play your favorite sport afterward, right?

If you could read your favorite novel for half an hour every evening before bed, dealing with your toddlers earlier wouldn't feel so unbearable.

If you had the tough conversation about that one toxic relationship, you'd have more courage to get to the gym, stick to a routine, and lose that extra weight. Working through relationships can be difficult and time-consuming, but often a first step is just opening the door to conversations you've been avoiding.

In this chapter, we're going to find some places where you can add some small amounts of energy to your life. That's right, I said *small*. I'm going to help you find the easy, small, and even *fun* ways you can add some net new energy into your life. Most of this will be so easy, you might find it silly. But that's the whole point of this book—homing in on the micro-changes that can lead to big impact. Sometimes that requires you to loosen up a little and be willing to try something new that might even make you feel a little awkward.

For instance, one of the energy-builders I usually share with clients is super easy and sounds childlike. It's to skip. Not like "skip leg day," or "skip that song you hate on Spotify," but literally skip.

Sounds crazy, right? Look, I get nervous just as much as the next guy. I've been pretty lucky—I've gotten to speak on some pretty big stages. And when I step onstage, I try to seem pumped up and ready to go.

What you may not know is that about thirty minutes before I walk onto that stage, I'm scared. Terrified, sometimes. I don't like the stages. I don't like the thought of all those people sitting there. I get the jitters, sweaty palms . . . you know, all that stuff. Sure, over time, *some* of that goes away, but if it were up to my nerves, half an hour before I step out onto the stage to speak, I'd be finding a reason to turn around and head back to my hotel. The reason I don't grab an Uber and disappear every time is what I do about ten minutes before I go out onstage.

I skip down the hall, like a child. (I'm happy my wife didn't see that before we got married!) Why does that work? Well, because *fixing physical posture* is one of the five micro-energy boosters. These boosters help us transform those low-energy moments in life into energized full engagement. We'll dive into each and learn how they can change our energy instantly. Take a look:

1. Posture pick-me-ups
2. Excitement anchors
3. Chargers who build you up

4. Customized rest
5. Finding confidence in a strong "why"

1. Posture Pick-Me-Ups

YOUR PHYSICAL POSTURE impacts your energy (and your confidence) more than you can imagine. World-renowned speaker Tony Robbins says it likes this: "Motion creates emotion." If you can get your blood moving differently—namely, in a more positive way—you'll start thinking more positively and feeling more positive.

In a study by social psychologist and author Amy Cuddy, two random groups of people were asked to give a saliva sample, and then to stand in either a "high-power pose" or a "low-power pose" for two minutes.[3] The researchers then took a second saliva sample after the pose. (Note to educators: Doing science with saliva would make science class so much more fun!) Cuddy found that people could *literally change their hormone levels with their poses.* "High-power poses" increased levels of testosterone (the hormone associated with feeling powerful and with assertiveness) and decreased levels of cortisol (known as the "stress hormone"). By contrast, "low-power poses" decreased levels of testosterone and increased levels of cortisol.

If there were a nickname for the hormones that are being released while I skip, I think they'd be the I'm-feeling-like-I'm-twenty-two-years-old hormones. You just can't help but feel energized when you're skipping. So, yes, my skipping routine (which I found by total accident) is backed by science.

And for all you skeptics out there: Once when I told an audience about my skipping routine, I ran into a tough-asnails coach afterward. This guy had taken his high school basketball team to five straight championships. The friend who'd invited me to the group described the coach as stone-cold and stoic, adding, "He never smiles. He doesn't laugh."

The coach heard every word of my talk on how energy influences our confidence, and then I bumped into him in the hallway afterward. Looking back, I think I probably expected him to—at best—shake my hand and say "Good work" before walking off. But that's not what happened. Mr. I've Never Smiled went, "I really enjoyed that presentation. That was some great stuff, Juan."

Do I smile? Do I wait for him to smile? Do we both smile? Do we skip the smile? I had a lot of ideas going through my head, but nothing could have prepared me for what I saw: The championship coach with ice in his veins turned around and—true story—skipped down the hallway, then turned around and came back. Then he looked at me and said, "Most of the time I'm asleep during these sessions, but you brought a great perspective to us all. I'm going to use this with my athletes."

Now, obviously, skipping isn't the only way to have a posture pick-me-up. Here are some other ideas:

- Stand tall, shoulders back.
- Puff out your chest when you feel defeated.
- Go for a quick walk outside to move *and* change your physical environment simultaneously.
- Throw on your favorite song and dance for a few minutes.

Or come up with your own idea, and don't worry how silly it might sound to anyone else. Randall, the Disney performer mentioned earlier, who couldn't dance his way into a jazz square (like, for real, he hid in the bathroom for half of his homecoming dance). And somehow the guy lands *a dancing role* in the cast at Walt Disney World (even though a choreographer once told him, "Wow. You really are that bad"). So, before he'd go out onstage and get paid to dance (I'm still laughing thinking how ridiculous this is, because he's awful—like, truly awful), he'd put on some Taylor Swift music. There he'd be in the back, a twenty-eight-year-old man jamming out to one of her songs to psych himself into doing something he was (and, indeed, should have been) insanely insecure about doing.

If you're looking for the less embarrassing version of this tool, you can try going for a brisk walk before that big presentation, swinging your arms back and forth, or just bouncing in place for twenty seconds.

A Few Other Childlike Activities You Can Do

IF I HAD labeled the first energy booster "act like a child," about nine-tenths of my guy friends would have skipped this section. Honestly, though, it does work. Numerous studies have concluded that play is a key ingredient in learning and productivity.[4] Here are a few other activities you can try:

1. Coloring (there's cool research on how it de-stresses, recharges you, etc.)
2. Doing a puzzle (there's research on how good it is for the brain)
3. Scheduling nap time for yourself
4. Playing a board game
5. Writing a letter to Santa

2. Excitement Anchors

I HAVE A friend, Tina, who landed a new job a couple of years back. It was taxing—lots of difficult responsibilities and tasks. But it wasn't a *bad* job; she actually enjoyed part of the work, the good pay, and the career she was building. The problem was that it was just tough. But she knew that merely because something's difficult, that doesn't mean you need to stop doing it.

Still, she needed to find some way to get through the tough parts week in and week out. So she tried an excitement anchor—something that makes you excited that goes on your calendar and helps give you energy *today*.

The cool thing about excitement anchors is that they're different for different people. Tina chose something simple— her weekly excitement anchor was watching *American Idol*. The show only came on once a week. So Tina would look forward to it every week as she toughed out a hard task or assignment at work. Amazingly, that energy was enough that even her team noticed.

Excitement anchors can be anything—a dinner date with a friend, a bike ride, a trip to Disney. They can be as big as a vacation or as small as listening to a podcast. What matters is that they're exciting to *you*.

Again, think about it—what if your *entire calendar* was chock-full of your favorite things every day, every week, every month?

- Getting your favorite drink at the local coffee shop
- Taking a thirty-minute walk, run, or bike ride
- Reading your favorite magazine or book
- Grabbing a treat from the bakery at the corner

- Pulling out your old skateboard or roller skates
- Doing an hour of your favorite art
- Taking a free class online to learn about a new topic you've been interested in

How you do it is up to you—you could decide to do the same thing every week (say, bowling night every Thursday), or you could set aside a day a week and just do something fun but mix it up. It doesn't even have to be so regular—maybe you're a pilot or a nurse and your schedule is never "regular." Just find the holes and plug them with a list of your favorite things.

I find it's easiest to do what Tina did—set a few things weekly—but the key is simple: When you look at your calendar, you should feel excited that this is your life.

A quick note: Excitement anchors don't have to be expensive, either in terms of your wallet or in terms of your time. Sure, if you've got the hours (and the dough), you can decide to start training for an Ultimate Fighting Championship bout forty hours a week and buy yourself a bunch of personal training sessions. But you can also find time in your day just to plug what you love into your routine.

One friend decided that his work—which in many ways he loved—was getting so stressful at one point that he almost didn't want to go to work. To make matters worse, he had no time left in his day after taking care of kids, work, and medical appointments. But then, by accident, he added an excitement anchor into his day. His car broke down, and out of necessity he went and bought a bike so that he could get to work, but guess what? *He loved it.* Biking relieved his stress and reinvigorated his energy for his career. Even after his car got fixed, he didn't stop riding his bike!

You may hate cycling. No sweat—find your own excitement anchor, whether it's your favorite TV show, a great latte, a new sport, or hang time with your favorite romance novel, and plug it into your calendar.

3. Chargers Who Build You Up

ENVIRONMENTS, PEOPLE, ACTIVITIES, tasks, and downtime do one of two things for us at all times—they either give us energy or take energy away.

And when it comes to *people*, I have names for these categories: *chargers* and *drainers*.

Let's take a look at my friend Stephen, for example. He is, without a doubt, a charger. When Stephen tells a story, he's having such a great time telling it, everyone else can't help but have a great time, too. His attitude ignites the physical space around him, arousing the same joy he's feeling in everyone else.

A drainer, on the other hand, is the person who, after you converse with them, you feel like you need a nap. We'll talk about them more in the next chapter. But, obviously, in an ideal world you'll spend less time with drainers. The antidote to their toxicity? People who charge you up.

I've got a great story about drainers and chargers. In the introduction, I told you about my high school English teacher Mrs. H., who gave such inspirational talks as "Juan, you're not an effective communicator" and "Some people were born with the gift of communication. You were not."

She was quite the lady. For a time, I believed her. I was ready to give up on the skills of speaking and writing forever.

So how did I end up here? Two chargers—my mother and another teacher, an amazing woman named Mrs. P.

Mrs. P. was your stereotypical drama teacher, but with an added dose of crazy encouragement. She actually told me that I should speak in front of people. She didn't tell me that I had an amazing ability with words, because I didn't. Instead, she told me that my message was on point, that my weakness was simply an opportunity for growth, and that I could improve if I wanted to. I didn't get good overnight. I took baby steps in drama class, Mrs. P. would encourage me more, and I'd feel more energized to try harder. Eventually I'd get to college and have the opportunity to speak in front of a thousand people, as you'll read later. At that point I thought about calling Mrs. H. just to let her know that the guy who she'd said would never be able to do mass communication was now about to speak in front of ten million people (I mean, I would have exaggerated the whole thing a little to her), but I was scared out of my mind. So instead of bragging to Mrs. H., I called Mrs. P., and she encouraged me about my upcoming gig.

The power of words is hard to overstate. Remember the psychologist Albert Bandura, whom we talked about earlier? He listed four major buckets that impact our self-confidence, and one of them is *words*. It's insane how much words affect us. With them, we can tear people down or build them up. It's why putting positive people in your life is so important.

The cool thing about being a charger is that this is one you can do for *other people*, too. And trust me, if you think surrounding yourself with chargers will bring you energy, *being* a charger will bring you ten times more.

Every Friday around 5:00 P.M., I log into Instagram to

keep up with friends and respond to any DMs. One Friday, I saw a message from Mitch:

> Mitch: Juan! I just wanted to thank you. I saw you speak a few years ago at a pretty pivotal time in my life. You helped me take action on my dream, so I just wanted to say thanks.

I told Mitch "Thank you," and then I noticed that he had one of the blue verification badges (before you could buy them for a monthly fee) on his profile. So, I clicked on his Instagram profile out of curiosity.

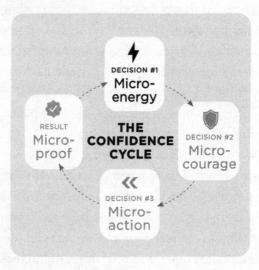

Turns out, Mitch played in the NHL.
I wrote him back instantly:

> Juan: The *NHL?!*

Mitch: Yeah! When I saw you speak, everyone in my life was telling me to quit hockey and be more "realistic." And honestly, I was about to. And then you came to speak. And you talked about letting go of what other people think and living your version of life. I decided to commit to hockey. So happy I did.

We all have had the experience of someone in our lives telling us what we can and can't do. They tell us to "be realistic" and "set achievable goals." The problem with that? Playing small. I'd rather you aim high and miss than aim low and hit. We need to find the people who build us up and support us striving toward big dreams. Decide what *you* want, commit to do whatever it takes to make it happen, and do it with the people in your corner.

4. Customized Rest

IN *PEAK PERFORMANCE,* Brad Stulberg and Steve Magness introduce a surprisingly simple formula: STRESS + REST = GROWTH.

When you think about it, this seems almost too obvious. Of course we need rest in between moments of intensity to restore our energy. In fact, without this rhythm, life would be either too easy or too overwhelming, both leading to less overall confidence. Elite athletes know how to do this—work hard and rest well. No one has more energy than these athletes, and their secret is rest. I can't tell you how many times I've been stumped on a work, school, or life problem, and a ten-minute walk around the building, a phone call to my friend, or just "sleeping on it" gives me the energy I need to move forward. But I think we can do better than intermittent breaks in our day.

In recent years, our society has developed a strange idea of what relaxing or unwinding looks like. We've taken the innuendo "Netflix and chill" and turned it literal. Now all we do at the end of a long workday is watch Netflix, or some other streaming service, and sit on our couch for two to four hours until it's time to go to bed. The next day, when we still feel our exhaustion and wonder why lying in a semi-vertical position for hours didn't replenish our energy, we opt for trying it again the next day, just to see if it'll work this time.

Watching TV or scrolling on our phones for a small amount of time may count as relaxing for a few of us. I wrote earlier about Tina, who used *American Idol* as her reward for the long weeks at her new job. But in general, most of us need something different.[5]

The key is to think about rest *intentionally* and *proactively*. Before it's time to rest, consider what you need to rest. This sounds very, very basic, but remember, we're trying to build a confident you by starting über-small. One way it starts is with rest.

Keep this simple and keep it *customized to you*. If you like to knit, gather all the items you need, make yourself a nice knitting basket, and put it somewhere easily accessible. If you know that going for a jog after work helps you unwind, get your jogging stuff out *before* work, with your shoes and clothes all ready to go.

Real rest—the restorative kind that combines with positive challenges to create energy—doesn't happen by accident. Real rest happens when we plan it out. When we're faced with a task and can't find the energy to confidently approach it, we need to recharge intentionally.

Here are a few things that many people find restful:

- Working out
- Meditating
- Working on a passion project
- Sketching or painting
- Gardening
- Reading
- Playing board games

5. Finding Confidence in a Strong "Why"

REMEMBER DEE FROM earlier? Recap: She grew up with hard-working parents who juggled multiple jobs just to put food on the table. Dee worked and worked and worked until she got enough money to buy her parents a house.

Most of these energy boosters are baby steps. If there is one that's a really big step, it's this one: *You've got to have a big "why."* For Dee, it was buying her parents a house. What's yours?

A "why" is truly important because some energy killers—like bad habits—are pretty darn difficult to get rid of. Another reason is that some tasks, such as difficult work assignments, becoming a new parent, making a tough phone call, or dealing with medical issues, may by their very nature suck energy out of us, but they're necessary. For that second group of issues, I say you should get a big "why." Think of how confident a mama bear is when protecting her young cubs. Suddenly, she isn't scared of anything. Think of that one crazy time in your life when you asked for the raise, hit "send," stood up to an expert, or demanded justice. In most of these cases, you suddenly became someone else in a crazy, confident moment, because what was on the line *mattered*.

Humans are pretty tough cookies. We can deal with an immense amount of difficulty *if* we have a good reason for it. Women go through some of the worst pain an individual can experience to give birth to their child—and then, miraculously, many will *repeat* that pain, voluntarily, because what's on the other side is their "why."

What's yours?

You may have already plugged this into your life's GPS and are ready for it. But a lot of people I've met don't really know what their "why" is. Why are you going to kick that bad habit? Why are you going to be a good spouse? Why do you want to lose weight?

Big problems require a big "why."

Confidence Cheat Sheet

- Five areas to find micro-energy boosts:

    1. **POSTURE PICK-ME-UPS.** Change your posture, skip around, do a little dance. These small things really matter!
    2. **EXCITEMENT ANCHORS.** Take your calendar out right now and look at the next week and month. Do you see activities that make you genuinely excited? If not, add some in!

3. **CHARGERS WHO BUILD YOU UP.** The converse of difficult people (drainers) is a few people who are insanely encouraging (chargers). Better yet, be someone else's charger!

4. **CUSTOMIZED REST.** Find (and plan for) what brings you joy every day, whether that's knitting, meditating, riding a bike, or arm-wrestling your older brother.

5. **FINDING CONFIDENCE IN A STRONG "WHY."** When things get really tough, a big "why" will help motivate you to stick it out.

- Too often we try to simply escape challenges, believing that all stress is bad. However, many challenges that create stress or difficulty are actually *good* for us, as long as they are combined with rest.
- Intentional rest > random screen time. The point isn't whether screen time is good or bad. The point is to proactively consider those restful, downtime items that bring *you* the most joy.

Micro-Step

I hope you picked up a few techniques in this chapter and the last that will help you up your energy game! Importantly, it really all comes down to your calendar. Maybe you're not a planning-type person, and that's OK. The question is: When you think about the next week and the next month, will you be involved in activities, events, meetings, and work that you're genuinely excited about? If we're honest, most of us don't have even two or three items we can look forward to.

Pull out your calendar right now and schedule at least one item every week, for the next ten weeks, that you're insanely excited about. These don't have to be complicated or expensive, and they don't have to require much time. They can be simple and varied—one week you could just set aside time to read your favorite book, and the next week it could be a two-day vacation. Or you could find a weekly event or activity that happens on a schedule (think church, a new dance class, or bowling night). You can be as grand or as minuscule as you want to be—but you must have one item every week to look forward to. If you can't get away from your house or work right now due to a baby, lack of money, or just a lot going on, that's OK. Pick something easy you can do that takes only a few minutes. But if you can't find half an hour a week to do something you love, you're headed toward trouble—*fast*. On the other hand, once your week starts to have something in it that you're excited about, I promise you that you'll show up better for your family, your work, and your whole life.

Plus you'll instantly find that you're a little bolder. And that's what we're talking about next.

4.

How to Overcome the
Five Energy Killers

———

The energy of your intention is
what determines your life.

—OPRAH WINFREY

OU PROBABLY HAVE BIG DREAMS AND GOALS FOR YOURSELF—
to be a writer, to be a speaker, or maybe just to learn to speak
up more at the dinner table. Whatever your goals are, this part
of the book should give you the energy to get started on them.

In the last chapter we learned how to get more energy into
your life. That with just a little bit of energy, you'll immediately feel more confident in what you're doing.

But now I want to plug the holes. I want to tell you how to
stop the five biggest energy suckers that keep tearing down
your excitement in life. Because if you can just find *one* of
these energy killers and get rid of it, it'll be like plugging a
huge hole in your energy pipes. Then, as you work to gain
more energy, you'll *actually get to keep it.*

Throughout this chapter, I want you to think of taking
back your energy from these energy killers and then redepos-

iting that energy into focus on your goals. You only have so much energy, and you should focus all of it where you actually want it to go, not on things that drain you unnecessarily.

So, without further ado (I've always wanted to say that!), here are the five major energy killers.

1. Toxic Physical Environments

I CAN BEAT Michael Phelps at a race.

In fact, so can you.

If Michael Phelps and I were racing, I'd just make one simple change: I'd go into a new environment, while he stayed in the pool. Namely, I'd leave the water and start jogging alongside him—actually, just quickly *walking* on dry land—and I'd easily beat the greatest Olympic swimmer of all time in a race.

That's the power of environment—same person, different environments, drastically different results.

Dr. Jordan Peterson talks extensively about cleaning your room. As he says, it's an externalization of your mind. A clean room makes you feel at peace, like your life is in order; a messy room makes you feel as if your whole life is in chaos. If your room is chaotic, it will eat at your confidence, and there's no way you're going to reach your goals if you feel like your room and your life are a chaotic mess.

When we think of our inner energy, often the first place we should look is *outside,* to see what factors around us are zapping our energy. But energy isn't just about cleanliness, or about how nice or fancy an environment is; it's about order, stability, and peace. I've walked into opulent homes that have immediately made me feel chaotic. Conversely, I've walked into more modest homes that smelled nice and were organized, making me instantly feel comfortable.

Much of this is objective: The human mind enjoys cleanliness over clutter and order over chaos. Some of it comes down to preference: One guy I know has to have excitement going on around him to work. So he goes to a local rock-climbing gym, uses their lobby to work on his laptop, and every couple of hours he hits a few walls. Why? For him, working in a cubicle in the local co-working space was sucking the life out of him. So, to boost his energy, he rid himself of that "toxic" environment.

Think about your two or three major touchpoints throughout the day (your bedroom, your living space, your working space). Are they clean and in order, with some items you enjoy, like artwork, pictures of your family, plants, or (if you're crazy) rock-climbing walls?

When I was moving recently, I didn't have my studio all set up at my new place, and it just felt *weird* doing virtual keynotes and coaching calls in makeshift setups. Luckily, a friend let me use her dedicated studio at a moment when I really needed it.

It's shocking to most people how their energy immediately goes up or down based on their physical environment, or how their work productivity is impacted by subtle changes in light, greenery, artwork, and decorations.

One Simple Question

GO THROUGH THE major spaces in your life and consider what's bringing you down. Do you work in a cold, drab office that you hate going to? What are your options for livening it up? Can you work from home, a local Starbucks, or a gym with a lobby? If working off-site isn't an option, spruce up your work space— a few dollars can go a long way for some plants and pictures. If your house is constantly messy, you have options—you can hire a cleaner or clean it up yourself on a regular schedule.

It doesn't really matter *how* you fix your toxic environment. The important thing is to take an inventory of your day, the places you go, and how you travel to work, and ask yourself an honest question: "Do these spaces make me feel alive?"

If the answer is no, write down one space you can fix today and one tweak you can make to brighten it up.

Our confidence in ourselves increases significantly when where we're living looks nice and clean. Immediately we'll have a better opinion of ourselves: "I'm a clean person. I have my life together." Plus plants, a few pictures, and other such things make us happier.

2. Negative Thoughts

MANY OF US speak very harshly to ourselves. Often, we may think one good thing about ourselves, but if we're honest, we're probably thinking negative thoughts at least three or four times as much.

What if you talked to your friends the way you think about yourself? Can you imagine if for every single nice comment you gave to your friend, you delivered *three or four* harsh criticisms? I'm going to write this out to show how absurd it would be.

One nice comment:

- "Hey, Juan, glad we got to hang out today."

Four criticisms:

- "Juan, your breath smells bad sometimes."
- "Juan, your wardrobe is out of date."
- "Juan, you aren't that great a writer."
- "Juan, you can be a pretty fearful guy over stupid things."

You know what's crazy about all those? A lot of them are true (I mean, everyone has bad breath sometimes), but can you *imagine* actually talking to someone like that? Of course not. It would be crazy.

Yet we talk to ourselves like that all the time.

You may have made mistakes. Your wardrobe may be out of date. But your emphasis on the negative aspects of your life is draining you.

The battle for your mind is a precious one. Perhaps it feels normal to pinpoint our worst insecurities because we are the ones who have to live with them. But what we don't realize is how these internal dialogues concerning our own worth are rewriting our personal views of ourselves. With every "I'm not _____ enough," we deplete the energy we need to think of ourselves in a positive way.

Then, of course, there's our negative thoughts about others. Our modern society has learned to bond over the worst aspects of human life, be it personal bad news, bad news from the world outside (such as plane crashes), or bad habits (like staying up too late scrolling Instagram). From this fascination with everything going wrong, we've developed a tendency to focus solely on mistakes. Take how we view celebrities: When we aren't applauding them for winning an Oscar or crushing it on the big screen, we gossip about them. A lot of publications have a dedicated gossip section. In fact, entire magazines are so full of gossip, it's now a *genre*.

Our minds, for whatever reason, are prone to look for the negative. When we post a photo or video, what do we notice first? The several (or millions, if your last name is Kardashian) likes and comments telling us how great we look, or the 1 or 2 percent of comments that are negative, telling us how we're not good enough in one way or another?

We underestimate the power of our own thoughts. According to an article published in the *Proceedings of the National Academy of Sciences,* "The human brain is just 2 percent of the body's weight, but 20 percent of its metabolic load, and 10 times more expensive [in terms of energy used] per gram than muscle."[1] Our mind is consuming *ten times* more energy than our muscles, because that's how much our brains matter.

Negative thoughts are an absolute energy killer.

And there's no way you're going to be the great person you know you can be if you let negative thoughts suck the life out of you.

Two Tips to End Negative Thoughts

YOU HAVE TO hunt negative thoughts with absolute tenacity, because for every one that gets away, you have a 95 percent chance of repeating it the next day. So, let's go hunting. There are lots of ways to combat negative thoughts, but to simplify it for you, I'll give you two of my favorites:

- **THE RUBBER-BAND TRICK.** One way therapists help their patients stop their negative thoughts is with a simple rubber band—put a rubber band on your wrist, and every time your mind starts heading down the wrong path, you give your wrist a little snap. Over time, you retrain your brain.

- **DO A SOCIAL MEDIA AUDIT.** Let's get real—a *ton* of our negativity comes from our social media likes and dislikes. Go through all the people you follow, and ask yourself, "Does following them bring me happiness?" If the answer is no, click that unfollow button.

Choose one of those and start it today so that you can work on clearing out those negative thoughts. Negative thoughts will never completely go away; that's because of how we are wired. The goal here is to notice when they show up and intentionally replace them with more empowering thoughts. The more you do this, the better you will become. Soon you will find yourself tipping the scales toward 80 percent of your thoughts being positive. Now *that* is a life worth pursuing.

3. Poor Habits

POOR HABITS—DRINKING HEAVILY, doomscrolling, staying up late, munching on chips—kill our energy. Fast.

We aren't dumb; we know some of those habits aren't sustainable over the long term. But often, instead of planning ways to get out of that lifestyle, we settle. We fall into daily rhythms that neither excite nor nourish our minds or bodies. We wake up feeling like we haven't gotten enough sleep, so we make coffee to fix it. Then we drive to work, and work until it's time to go home. After that we fill what's left of the day with whatever "relaxes" us. Then we do it all over again the next day.

We tell ourselves "we're doing our best," then commiserate with those who think negatively, which makes us feel better, but only temporarily.

The lifestyle that we dream about is possible, but that lifestyle often conflicts with the most prevalent energy killers: *inconsistent sleep, improper nutrition,* and *being sedentary.*

I get it—we all have our reasons for our vices. But this is where I give my "rituals over reasons" speech.

Rituals over Reasons

WE ALL HAVE "reasons" for our poor habits—our parents didn't train us, we don't have enough money, we hate our jobs, we're too exhausted, we have no friends, we have too many friends, we're unfulfilled, we have too many options, we don't have enough options, we're too bored, it's too hard . . . blah blah blah. Those are all the *reasons.*

But you've got to find your biggest, worst habit and eliminate it. And you do that with a *ritual*—an easily repeatable routine that replaces your "reason" with a better alternative.

- If you doomscroll every evening in bed, move your charger outside your room and make a simple rule: No phones in bed.
- If you don't drink enough water, set reminders on your phone.
- If you have struggles with your weight or fitness, find a program that you enjoy, and start small. It could be weightlifting, walking every morning, cycling to work, anything. Make it easy, make it fun, and make it a routine.

- If you never get out of your house, set aside an hour to plan out the next three months of weekly activities with your friends.

Now, this isn't a habits book. There are plenty of excellent books that deep dive into how habits can change your life. In fact, I highly recommend reading a book like *Atomic Habits* by James Clear after you finish this one.

But bad habits can be a big energy killer. Here's why. Habits are the little steps that allow you to reach your goals and keep promises to yourself. Let's say you've made a goal to get in shape, and maybe you want to hit the gym three days a week. If you've built a habit of going to bed at 9:00 P.M., you'll get enough sleep to wake up at 5:00 A.M. to hit the gym before work. That habit is a little stair step that lifts you up until eventually you reach your goal.

If, on the other hand, you doomscroll on social media until midnight, you probably won't feel like going to the gym at 5:00 A.M., and by not going to the gym consistently, you're breaking a promise to yourself—the promise to work out and get in shape.

Keeping promises to yourself provides *proof* that boosts your confidence ("Juan, look at you go! Hitting the gym at 5 A.M. every morning. We're crushing it!"). Breaking promises to yourself destroys that proof ("Juan, you're lazy. How can you deliver a deal-closing presentation when you can't even stick to your word?"). Everything in your life is either building or depleting your confidence, so make sure you keep your promises to yourself. Habits are the key to doing that.

THE NEXT TWO ENERGY KILLERS

THE THREE ENERGY killers we've discussed so far are ones you can mostly get rid of (I mean, no one really needs a messy room or an addiction to social media), but the next three energy killers are a little trickier—you can't just "get rid" of overworking, for instance. Why? Well, you may love your job. Quitting could be worse than overworking. So, when we discuss these next three energy killers, note that how you handle is less "eliminate" and more "navigate," a technique I'll discuss.

4. Drainers

WE MENTIONED DRAINERS and chargers in chapter 3. Chargers give you energy, and drainers leave you needing a nap. In some social circles, drainers are called "EGRs," for "extra grace required." They complain. Nothing in their life has ever gone right, or seemingly will ever go right. The trash collector didn't pick up the trash, the spouse was late to their dinner date, and while the weather is sunny today, that just means it'll rain tomorrow.

You may have heard at some point, "You are the average of the five people you spend the most time with." If your energy reflected the energy of those five people, how would your life look?

Navigate, Don't Eliminate

I GET IT—YOU can't just remove certain people from your life completely. You may be thinking of a toxic person right now who's a family member, a co-worker, or someone else that you simply can't cut completely out of your life. I get that.

Instead, think of how you can *navigate* those people. If there's someone in your life that you truly can't avoid entirely, here are some tips:

- Decrease the interactions you have with them.
- Remind yourself ahead of time to control the topic of conversation.
- Choose a new environment (sometimes when you put a drainer into a different atmosphere, they transform).
- Have a timed escape plan (if you must meet this person, have another appointment that starts afterward).

Jeremy is a master at dealing with drainers. For instance, he strives to include his own mother in his children's (her grandchildren's) lives, but she doesn't share his family values. So, Jeremy has set up nightly "read-alongs" for his kids, which allow him to give Grandma and grandbabies some time together. But this also allows Jeremy to control the environment (she calls them on Zoom to read them their book), the topic (he picks the books), and the time (as soon as the book's over, he says, "It's time for bed!").

There are some people in your life you can step away from today and you'll probably never regret it. With others it takes some creativity to learn how to navigate the relationship. But with a little proactive thinking, there's usually a way to limit their negative impact on your energy.

Pick one drainer in your life and select one of the tips I

gave (choose a new environment, have an escape plan, control the conversation) to try out the next time you see them.

5. Stress and Burnout

AHH . . . STRESS. ANOTHER tricky one. Because *stress* can be good, in fact, there is a name for good stress: "eustress." It's a real thing; I'm serious.

What happens when you go to the gym? You put your muscles under stress. What happens when you force yourself to study just a little bit longer? You force your mind into stress. Without this stress, muscles wouldn't grow, minds wouldn't sharpen. If we avoided all stress, everyone would be weak and dull.

Good stress is "associated with positive outcomes . . . [and] unlike distress, eustress is typically associated with feelings of excitement and challenge rather than anxiety or fear."[2] When we undertake a new job, engage in a lively debate, or prepare for a difficult exam, our heart rate is elevated, we're more likely to sweat, and we might feel more nervous than usual. But that's not inherently negative—we're simply pushing our boundaries beyond their current edges.

You know that feeling of nervousness you get before you do something new or in front of others? That little nervousness is pointing you in the direction of where you need some growth or where you can extend your comfort zone. If you were to live your life solely within your comfort zone, you wouldn't be reading this book right now. The fact that you're doing so means you're reaching the outer boundary of who you are at present, and it indicates what you are capable of.

The problem isn't with stress itself but with a lack of *rest* in between stresses. You don't go to the gym for twenty-four hours straight; you go for an hour, then rest. Preferably, you rotate which muscle groups you work out every day.

Too often we overuse stress and pour it on our lives without any breaks or rest in between. We're constantly stressed, with little rhythm and no intermittent celebrations.

The same is true with burnout. I put these two together because while they are different in nature, the solution is the same for both. Stress and burnout have this in common: They can both come from too much of a good thing. Stress often comes from pushing ourselves beyond our comfort zone, and burnout comes from work.

We live in a time that glorifies "hustle until you're worth $10 million" and "sleep when you're dead." So, we continue the hustle well beyond our capacity, eliminating rest, opting for pick-me-ups instead, which increase caffeine addiction and mindless scrolling (bad habits that you now know are also energy killers).

What we forget is that humans have an incredible capacity for performance, stress management, and productivity, but— and yes, there is a but—*we need rest.*

A colleague of mine, Ed, used to come into work after a night out and brag about how he only needed four hours of sleep each night and still could work efficiently. He also claimed he could do CrossFit four times a week without needing a rest day in between. While at first there was some humor in his bragging routine, within six months he had quit his high-paying job, stopped going to CrossFit, and gained thirty pounds; he was unrecognizable. Despite his good intentions to have fun, take care of his body, and support his lifestyle, he burned himself out before ever reaching his goal.

As mental health and psychology author Brad Stulberg writes, "Studies show that [people] respond to stress by becoming stronger—[if] the period of stress is followed by adequate rest and recovery."[3] Ed's lifestyle was founded on improvement but neglected to have a balance between stress and rest. In Ed's world, rest equaled online shopping during lunch breaks and grabbing drinks after a long workday. Yet neither of these activities promoted true energy renewal.

What he needed was *rest*. True *rest*oration.

So, what's the solution here?

You need to build energy so you can build confidence. And that means you need to get rid of these last two energy killers.

Resting isn't just lying around and doing nothing. So, on your next day off, don't just "do nothing." Do something truly restorative. Make a list of ten things you find restorative and pick a few to do on your next day off.

Here's a list to get you inspired:

- Try a new coffee shop
- Go hiking
- Take a nap
- Do date night
- Play tennis
- Order in and watch a movie
- Read a book
- Bake brownies
- Get together with friends
- Lie in the sun
- Play board games
- Get in an ice bath (just me?)

ENERGY: THE SECRET
WEAPON TO CONFIDENCE

WE'RE CLOSING OUT the energy section of the Confidence Cycle, and I want to remind you how powerful energy can be. Often we are capable of more, but doing "more" sounds like a headache. We lack motivation not because we aren't capable but because we aren't energized. It's not that we're working too hard; it's that we don't have enough energy to keep us going. It's not that we can't achieve the goal; it's that we haven't directed sufficient energy toward it. I hope this chapter has sparked you to think a little bit more about energy.

You may have big goals on Monday, but then suddenly it's Tuesday and the kid's sick, the spouse is upset at you, and the boss is ticked. You're supposed to give a presentation that would be a huge step toward your career goals, but now you're not feeling very confident. Instead of thinking, *I need more confidence to achieve my goals,* stop and think, *Well, here's what I have to look forward to this week . . .*

If you still can't think of what you have to look forward to, go back and reread chapter 3. Starting with courage isn't going to cut it. You need to have *energy* in your physical environment, in the people you're hanging out with, and in your calendar. You don't have to have it all perfectly worked out, but you've got to be able to look at your life and feel excited if you're ever going to reach your goals.

Dan Martell, author of the *Wall Street Journal* bestseller *Buy Back Your Time,* has a lot of tough things on his plate. At any given time, he's writing his next book, managing one of his dozen companies, handling multimillion-dollar deals, speaking at a conference, or hiring or training one of his executives. His day is stacked with back-to-back intensive meetings. But where he gets the energy to face all this is pretty simple to see if you look at his calendar. Every day is filled with things Dan enjoys:

- Time in the morning to "create with the Creator," where Dan draws, writes, and thinks of new business ideas
- Weekly, scheduled dinner dates with his wife
- Wakeboarding with his two boys
- Hiking with his dog, Blaze

At any given moment, whether in the middle of a tough meeting, after a failed business deal, or following a book deal that went sideways, Dan can glance at his calendar and see that within a day he'll be getting to draw. Within a week he'll be on a date with his wife. Within a month he'll be wakeboarding or skiing with his kids. In fact, Dan takes this to a whole new level because a lot of times he does stressful things *while doing something he loves.* For example, Dan has been known to take meetings while hiking or working out. Instead of waiting until after work to do something he loves, he's doing it while he's working. That's constant energy, supplying him constant sparks to start a new Confidence Cycle.

Now, be honest—if I were to ask *you* what you're looking forward to this week or this month, what would you say? Is your calendar full of things you love, or is it full of things you hate doing? Are you genuinely excited about your week and your relationships, or do you dread the upcoming meeting with "that" person? Are you terrified of "that" task you'll have to perform?

I'm not suggesting you quit all your responsibilities. In fact, having more energy will allow you to show up *more* for the people in your life and for the tasks (even the difficult ones) you need to perform as a responsible adult. But just think about it.

- If you had more excitement in your life, how much more confident would you feel?
- If your calendar were full of things you loved instead of hated, how much more likely would you be to succeed?
- If you woke up every day full of anticipation about the day, how much more productive would you be?

That's what energy does, and that's exactly why energy has a huge target on its back.

Remember—this is about *micro*-doses. Find one or two things you can employ, and go get that energy.

Confidence Cheat Sheet

- Too many people attempt to change with motivation and willpower alone. But by themselves, these are temporary solutions. However, if you manage the availability of energy in your life, you can start a full revolution of the Confidence Cycle.
- There are five major energy killers:

    1. Toxic physical environments
    2. Negative thoughts
    3. Poor habits

4. Drainers

5. Stress and burnout

- The first three (toxic physical environments, negative thoughts, and poor habits) should all be mostly *eliminated*.
- One tactic you can use to eliminate an energy killer—especially a poor habit—is "rituals over reasons." This is a practice in which you take a bad routine and replace it with a good one—something easy (and preferably fun) that you can replicate *instead* of the behavior you wish to eliminate.
- The final two energy killers—drainers and stress/burnout—must be dealt with more delicately. (For example, you can't simply cut all stress out of your life, nor would you want to.)
- To deal with drainers, use the "navigate, don't eliminate" strategy. Proactively consider how you can limit your interactions with toxic people by controlling the scene, topic, and timeline (have an escape route available). The key is being *proactive*. Consider how you'll deal with people who are toxic but with whom you must interact.

Micro-Step

I want you to follow a simple three-step process to help you find the one energy killer that is really holding you back.

1. **DO AN ENERGY AUDIT.** Go through the five energy killers and give each one a score from 1 to 10 based on what that energy killer is doing in your life. A 1 means

the energy killer can't get you. A 10 means that energy killer has you dead in its sights. It's like golf—you're hoping for as low a score as possible.

2. **FIND THE ENERGY KILLER WITH THE HIGHEST SCORE.** Which energy killer is costing you the most energy right now?

3. **DETERMINE HOW TO SOLVE THE PROBLEM.** If you're dealing with any of the first three energy killers (toxic environments, negative thoughts, or poor habits), you'll likely want to use some version of "rituals over reasons." If your biggest energy villain is currently one of the other two, you'll probably need to use "navigate, don't eliminate," or you may come up with your own creative solution. The point is to *find the target* and then *fight back.*

Micro-Courage

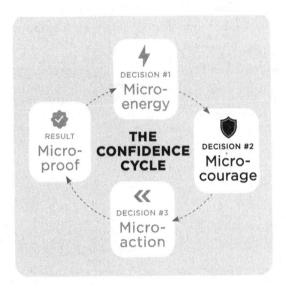

COURAGE: *The bravery that bridges energy and action.*

You start the Confidence Cycle the moment you find some energy in your life—with a clean room, scheduling a weekly dinner date with your best friend, joining a running club, putting something on your calendar that you enjoy. When you're able to anticipate something that brings you joy, you'll immediately feel more confident about your life.

You could stop there. But assuming you have a vision in

mind of who you really want to be—a better writer, the CEO of your own company, or simply someone who doesn't have as much social anxiety—that will take more effort. You'll need to eventually take micro-action toward your future vision.

For that, you'll need both energy *and* courage. Not the kill-a-mountain-lion kind of courage, but a micro-dose of courage to complete your micro-action.

And that's what you'll find in the next two chapters: that courage is the bridge between energy and action.

5.

"I'm Not There, *Yet*"

If something in you yourself says "you aren't a painter"—it's then that you should paint . . . and that voice will be silenced.

—VINCENT VAN GOGH

Y OU'RE ALWAYS TELLING YOURSELF A STORY.

In a now-famous experiment, psychologists Fritz Heider and Marianne Simmel took a group of people and showed them an animation of moving shapes—a couple of triangles and a circle moving around on a screen. When asked what they saw, almost everyone had concocted a wild story. Some thought the smaller triangle was protecting the circle from the bigger triangle, which was the bully. Others thought that the circle must represent a damsel in distress and the triangles were fighting over her. One even interpreted the large triangle as a witch trying to catch two children.

The truth is, there wasn't much to these shapes. They were just moving around on a screen. But what the psychologists discovered is that all humans are deeply connected to story: "Humans have a strong tendency to impose narrative even on displays showing interactions between simple geometric shapes."[1] In other words? We're hardwired to believe in a story, one that usually involves a hero fighting for a cause.

What most of us don't realize is that as we go through the day and experience failures and successes, these aren't just a collection of singular, disconnected events. Well, even if they *are,* our mind doesn't interpret them that way. Our mind *will* make a story out of it. And if we're not careful, that story is "Look at how many times you failed. You're a failure" or "See, the world is just against you. You're not one of the special ones."

Author Donald Miller, who has written multiple *New York Times* bestsellers, has based the second part of his career on this philosophy. After years of research for his other books, he concluded that we all have a deep desire to be the hero of our own story, and he now shows businesses how to make their customers the hero of that story (you can check out how he does this in his amazing book *Building a StoryBrand: Clarify Your Message So Customers Will Listen*).

I hope you're catching what I'm pitching—your brain is on the hunt for a story. And if you don't give it one, it'll create one for you. In fact, I bet it already has . . . and it's probably not a pretty one. Maybe right now your story is "I've been out of the workforce raising kids for five years, so there's no way I could get my great corporate job back." Maybe it's "I'm forty-one years old and single—no one wants to marry me." Or even "I'd love to run my own business, but my old boss just went bankrupt and it's really shaken me up."

It's hard to be confident when this is your story. So, why not take control of the narrative and tell a different one?

REFRAMING YOUR FLAWS

IN THE 1960S, DC Comics had taken center stage in the fight for superheroes, and they might have won the overall war with their biggest competitor, Marvel, if it hadn't been for one man, Stan Lee. Comic books had been popular for a long time before Stan Lee showed up, but today nearly every comic book character you can think of has been influenced by his ideas.

See, before Lee, superheroes were just that: super and heroic. Some people enjoyed these perfect characters with (literally) out-of-this-world abilities. But Lee believed superheroes shouldn't be so perfect—he believed they should be relatable figures who have struggles and pitfalls that readers could empathize with. (His editors thought he was crazy, and almost didn't let him publish many of his ideas!)[2] Eventually, Lee and others introduced heroes like the Amazing Spider-Man, Captain America, and Iron Man, whose real-life problems "defied the superhero archetype."[3] Interestingly, most of us today now perceive the superhero archetype as a superhero with some sort of weak spot.

Lee knew something his editors didn't grasp at first: Humans enjoy stories where the hero has a struggle to overcome.[4] If Spider-Man weren't a teenager limited by his family dynamics, his capabilities and triumphs wouldn't be astonishing. If the Hulk had been able to dominate his anger, you wouldn't sympathize with his fight for self-control. We love to see heroes win, not because they are effortlessly courageous or magically talented but because they fought their demons and triumphed over their weaknesses. In our minds—whether we realize it or not—that gives us hope: *If they can conquer their demons, maybe I can conquer mine and unleash my own potential.*

By introducing flawed characters through Marvel super-heroes, Lee unintentionally helped us see ourselves in them—inspiring us to discover our own hero capabilities. We know we are meant for great things, but what gets in the way for us all is that voice in our head. We want to start the business, get into great shape, build amazing friendships, but the inner critic makes us stop dead in our tracks. Consumed by self-doubt, we fail to reach our goals not because we weren't destined for greatness but because we don't believe we have what it takes to overcome the obstacles to making our dreams happen.

Here's what blows my mind, and I hope yours, too: We want superheroes to have problems that they overcome (that's how we relate to them), but when *we* have struggles, we believe that we're failures.

We tell ourselves, "Pain is bad, failure is evil, and if I lose, I'm a loser." Do we always know this narrative is happening? No, but if we're not actively telling ourselves a different narrative, then the narrative "I'm a loser" will automatically play every time you lose:

- You start a project but lose motivation: point for self-doubt
- You get fired from your job: point for self-doubt
- Your best friend disapproves of your significant other: point for self-doubt
- You drop a pass during a key moment in your basketball game: point for self-doubt

We internalize these points over time, and they seem to tell us we're failures. But here's what's wild: No matter how many times Rocky falls to an opponent, we just want him to win the next match. We don't think Peter Parker is a total loser because he struggles with his family dynamics. We don't hate Iron Man even though he can (at times) have a big ego. We aren't angry with Captain America even though he's a hopeless romantic who can't be with Peggy Carter. And (for DC fans) we aren't angry with Superman because of his vulnerability to kryptonite, or with Batman because he's not *really* a superhero.

Do you get that? We are holding ourselves to a higher standard than superheroes. When you think about it like that, it's ridiculous, right? It's so ironic that we say, "I screwed up, which makes me a failure, and failures will always screw up," but then, simultaneously, *all* our favorite superheroes have weaknesses, failures, and soft spots, and we believe they will prevail over those hurdles.

And if mythological superheroes aren't your thing, take a look at some of the failures of real-life heroes:

WALT DISNEY: In 1919 his editor told him he "lacked imagination and had no good ideas." He then received over three hundred rejections from bankers because his animation idea seemed crazy.

OPRAH WINFREY: She was born in 1954 and had to overcome much hardship and rejection in her early life because she was a Black woman. After finally becoming a co-anchor on Baltimore's WJZ-TV, she got fired from this dream job. She decided to set up her own show and is now a self-made billionaire.

GIANNIS ANTETOKOUNMPO: Originally a stateless child of Nigerian immigrants, Antetokounmpo is now one of three brothers from his family who have played in the NBA. Giannis's parents moved from Africa before he was born. Without proper paperwork, they couldn't find steady work until a scout bumped into Giannis and his brothers. The scout offered to get his parents better jobs *if* they allowed him to train their children. They agreed. Today, he's one of only three basketball players—the others being LeBron James and Kareem Abdul-Jabbar—to win MVP twice before the age of twenty-six.[5]

STEPHEN KING: The author of *The Shining* used to live in a trailer, drive a broken-down Buick, and work as a gas pump attendant in the 1970s. During that period, he was writing his first novel, *Carrie*. Thirty publishers rejected the book. Many times King thought of putting his dream aside and accepting his life as it was, but he kept on going. Today, he has sixty-one novels and countless awards in his pocket. The *New York Times* bestseller list has featured more than thirty of his works.

JEFF BEZOS: It was the summer of 2015, and Jeff Bezos was ready to take on the iPhone with Amazon's Fire Phone. The phone was originally priced at $199, but after lackluster sales the phone was soon going for a buck. *Fortune* declared, "Amazon's stumble with the Fire is a major setback for the online retailing giant."[6] A *Fast Company* story on the product failure began with one question: "What the hell happened?"[7] *Wired* magazine wasn't even surprised, publishing an article headlined "The Amazon Fire Phone Was Always Going to Fail."

That last one really gets me, particularly because of what Bezos said during an interview: "If you think that's a big failure, we're working on much bigger failures right now."[8]

I know what you're thinking: *Yeah, that's all well and good for these über-successful folks, but that's because they are already confident. I'm scared to death of my failures!*

Well, that makes sense. But let me point something out to you—if *they* failed, then you are definitely going to fail.

Let me repeat that: You're definitely going to fail.

If superheroes failed, you're going to fail.

If Superman is vulnerable to kryptonite, you're vulnerable to your kryptonite.

If Jeff Bezos made bad financial decisions, you're going to make bad financial decisions.

If people treated Oprah Winfrey badly, they'll treat you badly.

Wow, Juan. Thanks for the words of encouragement.

Here's my point—I can't change the fact you, me, Oprah Winfrey, and everyone else on earth has failed and will fail. A *ton*. Heck, religions have stories of when *gods* failed. The truth is, failure isn't just a small part of life we can wish away or bury. The human condition is the story of failure. And in fact, *avoiding* failure—which isn't really possible anyway—is actually a horrible idea. Science backs this up.

The Kellogg School of Management conducted a study on scientists whose research had been successful over time, and here's what they found: The earlier professionals failed, the more likely they were to succeed later in life.[9]

Did you catch that? Let me put it in a hot take you can post on Instagram for all your friends to disagree with before you drop the research:

Failure = success.

The researchers decided to test their findings by using data from an odd group of people—terrorists. (Yeah, I know. Kinda weird!) The researchers used their earlier findings on failure to analyze over 170,000 terrorist attacks, and what they found was that terrorists who'd "failed" earlier became "successful" later on. Then they looked at data from successful venture capitalists. Same result: Those who fail earlier are much likelier to be successful later. The takeaway? "Every winner begins as a loser," notes the lead researcher, Yang Wang.[10]

OK, let's recap.

1. You're going to fail.
2. But that's OK because failure is the path to success.

So, how does all of this relate to confidence?

If you think failing makes *you* a failure, it will be pretty hard to build confidence. Instead of failing and thinking we're failures, we need to reframe the story to something different: "I failed. That's great! That's one step closer to success." Or as Thomas Edison is reputed to have said, "I have not failed 10,000 times—I've successfully found 10,000 ways that won't work."[11]

The most courageous people aren't those who naturally have a ton of courage; it's those who understand that failure is part of the process.

Think about it this way: If I hid a $100 bill under one of ten cups and said you had ten chances to find it, would you be disappointed if, after the first nine times, you *didn't* find it? Of course not. You'd actually be excited the more times you failed, knowing that the next time actually had a higher likelihood of success. In real life, you don't know how many times you're going to fail. It could be ten, a hundred, or half a million. But every time you fail, you can tell yourself that you're simply closer to success. And you can say that to yourself because it's true.

Reframing your failures is crucial because it allows you to keep up your courage. And remember, we need courage because it's the bridge between energy and action when building confidence. So, *specifically*, how can we do that?

"I'M NOT THERE, *YET*"

NOW, I WANT to be super-duper clear: I'm *not* suggesting that we give ourselves participation trophies, pretending that failures are successes. Pretending that you succeeded when you failed does nothing to increase your confidence. It makes you *unable* to handle life's realities.

The U.S. Navy SEALs, one of the toughest groups of men in the world, saw a recent plunge in the percentage of people who made it past a certain stage of the difficult SEAL training program. What was the issue? They commissioned a military report, and here's what they found.

The newer generation (Gen Z) had the highest level of physical fitness they'd ever seen coming into Navy SEAL training. However, they had a *lower* level of mental toughness. When things got hard, they bailed. And that's why they couldn't make it past a certain stage.[12] Similarly, Harvard doesn't want students who've never experienced failure. Failure, disappointment, rejection, an acknowledged mistake—these are what make you stronger. You learn from failures, and then you try again.

In recent years, we've slid into an odd type of extremism: Either you will never be enough, or you will always be enough. You'll never make your fitness goals unless you go to the gym five times a week—but if you *don't* go five times per week, you might as well not go at all, right? If you're a stay-at-home parent, don't let your kids watch TV, ever, or else you'll affect their brain development. But once they start watching TV . . . well, they might as well watch it while they eat dinner, snack on their dessert, and maybe on their way to the car, too. We either need to be gold medalists or pretend that winning doesn't matter at all.

As a result, in some areas we're insane perfectionists, while in others we've given up. *What if, instead of being so extreme, we strive for greatness but acknowledge that we may not be there, yet?* Similar to reframing our flaws, using "yet" allows us to change the story that plays over and over in our heads, the story that either boosts or crushes our courage:

- "I haven't lost all the weight I want to, *yet*."
- "I haven't achieved weekly date night with my spouse, *yet*."
- "I haven't kicked that bad habit, *yet*."
- "I haven't got the promotion I want, *yet*."
- "I haven't written that bestselling novel, *yet*."

That simple word "yet" is the difference between a failure derailing the Confidence Cycle and completing a revolution around it. Speaking of revolutions . . .

REVOLUTIONIZING THE REVOLUTION

IN 1775, GEORGE Washington was appointed commander in chief of the Continental Army. At the time, Washington had the most military experience in the country, but it wasn't exactly *good* experience—he'd "inadvertently started the French and Indian War in 1754," and then proceeded to lose most of the major battles in the war he accidentally started. Probably not unsurprisingly, he resigned that original military posting in 1758.[13] But then suddenly—perhaps because Washington was willing to work without getting paid—the soon-to-be United States Congress put all their faith in him and proceeded to start a war with the greatest military might the world had ever seen: the British. Most of that first year, 1776, went exactly as you might expect a war of unpaid farmer-soldiers to go against a professional military with more guns, ammo, and experience. Basically, Washington was getting his American butt kicked.

Washington spent most of 1776 just trying to hold down the fort (literally, several forts) in New York City. One after another, forts kept falling to the British, and to save the remainder of his troops, Washington retreated once, twice, three times . . . He'd basically trained North America's greatest track stars. They'd see a redcoat and run in the other direction, eventually all the way to Pennsylvania.

He finally decided that it was time to do something, so his American boys mounted up and crossed the Delaware River on Christmas day to attack an enemy he'd previously been running away from.

Washington didn't allow his former failures to make him into a failure. He took control of the narrative (for himself and his troops) and decided to have a victory.

But that reframing was his *choice:* "I haven't won, *yet.*" If, instead, Washington had allowed his failures to make him think that he was a failure, he'd have essentially been sabotaging his own revolution around the Confidence Cycle—and, in a sense, the entire American Revolution!

Here's what a failure does when we don't take control of our own narrative:

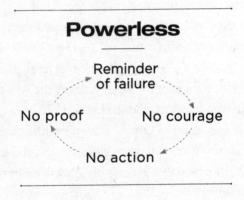

What a failure does when we do take control of our own story:

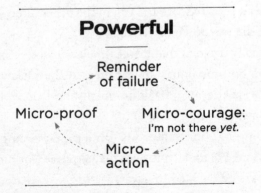

DIVING WITH SHARKS

LAST YEAR, MY WIFE, Gaby, and I visited Hawaii. She had the idea of going open-water shark diving. Naturally, I asked, "Why on earth would we do that?" But she had already booked it, and it was non-refundable.

When the day arrived, we traveled two hours from Honolulu to the North Shore, on the other side of the island of Oahu. When we got to the marina, I saw a quartet of twenty-somethings doing yoga beside a 1990s fishing boat. I went up to them and asked, "Is this Deep Blue Eco Tours?" to which they replied, "Yeah, totally." *Oh, boy.*

So we got in this old fishing boat with three Australian tourists and the dive team. The plan was to get out to a buoy three miles from the coast, lure the sharks by mimicking the movements of a crab boat so that the sharks would think it was time to eat, then we'd all jump in the water, led by the yoga crew of deep-sea philosophers. I thought, *So far, this sounds like a terrible plan.*

The swells got up to six or seven feet high, and Gaby and I were drenched head to toe. As we got closer to the buoy, the diving instructor laid out three rules for success:

- *Rule #1: When you're ready to get into the water, don't jump in; you'll mimic food. Just slide in.* I didn't really grasp the difference between jumping and sliding, but sure, that seemed fine.
- *Rule #2: Always maintain eye contact with the sharks.* But didn't sharks have eyes on either side of their head? And I was wearing goggles. How the heck—

- *Rule #3: When you're in the water, do not swim above, below, behind, on the side of, or directly in front of the sharks.* What else was left?

Of course, it sounded like we could have avoided rules 1 through 3 with rule 0: Never get in the water with sharks. But what did I know? I didn't even do yoga.

While we were being enlightened about the three ways to feel safe when diving with apex predators, I leaned over to the photographer and asked, "Have you had any accidents?" Without missing a beat, he replied, "We have a pretty good record." Well, I sure hoped this was going to be a pretty good day.

Mimicking the movements of a crab boat, which would signal to the sharks that it was time to eat, the captain moved the boat forward and backward, producing whitewater. Pretty soon, ten or more sharks started circling us, thrashing their tails against the sides of the boat. I ran through the three rules over and over again in my head as we prepared to jump—wait, no, *slide*—into the water. I looked at Gaby, who was as cool as a cucumber, and said, "OK, babe, you go ahead." She looked at me and said flatly: "You're going, too. You're the *confidence* guy, remember?"

I said a prayer to the shark gods and forced myself into the water. I pulled my goggles down just in time to notice dozens of sharks encircling me, some five feet below, others twenty-five feet down and just barely visible by their ominous silhouettes. Soon Gaby got in with the three Aussies. Every fifteen seconds or so, I turned to check on her, making sure she was safe and that I wouldn't die alone.

Forty-five minutes went by, and suddenly I couldn't see her. I'd lost her. I turned around, seeing nothing but the sharks and more blue ocean. I popped up from the water, but it was windy and the swells were so high that I couldn't even see the boat. Panic rose in my chest. I took my goggles off and tried to find the boat. After a few minutes, the swells died down, and at last I saw Gaby and everyone else safely in the boat. They had all left me. I finally swam back to the boat—all limbs intact, I might add.

To everyone else, the sharks were amazing and the waves were beautiful. (Probably most of them had a good laugh at my expense, too.) But the most interesting thing to me was what this whole experience taught me about confidence.

Now, it's true that I wasn't exactly a knight in shining armor. To be frank, I was nervous about the whole experience. But now *I* get to decide how this story goes. On one hand, I can tell the same story that my brain will tell me if I do nothing:

Juan acted scared → Juan is a fearful person → Juan can't be courageous

Or I can tell myself an entirely different story, one that's also true:

I jumped in the water with sharks → I was scared, but I did it anyway → Juan is a badass

Do you see how much I can change my confidence in myself just by how I tell this story? We haven't even talked much about the next two phases of the confidence cycle, which involve action and proof, but you can already see this all start working together:

Juan's Sharky Confidence Cycle

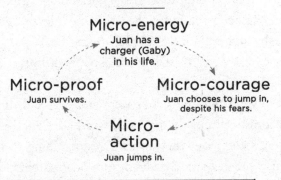

Micro-energy
Juan has a charger (Gaby) in his life.

Micro-courage
Juan chooses to jump in, despite his fears.

Micro-action
Juan jumps in.

Micro-proof
Juan survives.

Did I have fear? Sure. Did George Washington make mistakes? Absolutely. Do superheroes have faults? Of course they do (thanks in large part to Stan Lee).

But heroes aren't the ones without mistakes or fears. They're the ones who seize the story and tell it correctly.

Confidence Cheat Sheet

- Humans are hardwired to frame everything that happens to them (or anyone else) as part of a larger narrative.
- We all have a deep-seated connection with flawed characters who achieve greatness because deep down *we see our flaws and we hope we can achieve greatness in spite of them.*
- Failure is unavoidable. You *will* fail.
- Without proactive thought, most of us will (at least subconsciously) frame our experiences in a negative light—"I failed, therefore I'm a failure"—or, at the other extreme, we

will frame failure as if it doesn't matter (participation trophies).

- The correct way to view flaws, failures, or weaknesses is with a micro-shift: "I'm not there, *yet*."

Micro-Step

We're going to find all the ways in which you've been (probably accidentally) believing that your failures *make you* a failure. I want you to take some time with this one (set aside at least sixty minutes; you'll need it).

———

STEP 1: Write down your ten biggest failures that still haunt you. These could be one-off failures ("I went bankrupt") or habitual failures ("I cannot stop smoking cigarettes" or "I always yell when I get angry").

STEP 2: Add the word "yet" to each of the failures (you may have to rephrase it slightly). "I went bankrupt *because I'm not great with money, yet.*" "I cannot stop smoking cigarettes, *yet.*" "I haven't learned to control my tone, *yet.*")

STEP 3: Tape the list to your bathroom mirror. Try saying it to yourself (or at least thinking it) while you're brushing your teeth every morning *until you believe it.*

Now, the next time you catch yourself thinking that you're a failure, or that you can't do something or overcome a problem, remember: Add the word "yet."

---

* If you don't brush your teeth, wait for my next-next book: *32 Reasons to Scrub Those Pearly Whites.*

6.

The Opponents

———

Courage is the most important of all the virtues,
because without courage you can't practice
any other virtues consistently.

—MAYA ANGELOU

T'S 2010, MY SOPHOMORE YEAR OF HIGH SCHOOL. AT THIS POINT in my life, I was one of the least confident people you could ever meet. On top of that, I was overweight.

Every day, I saw my crush, Brittany, in the hallways at school and never said one word to her. She never noticed me, and I almost didn't want her to.

Some days I'd stop by my favorite drive-through coffee shop before school. One morning I pulled up and was about to place my regular order when I heard a new voice come through the speaker.

"Welcome! What can I get for you?"

I froze. It was Brittany. My mind began to formulate all the possible responses. Then my gut flipped as she repeated her question.

"Hello? Can I get you anything?"

I had no idea what to say. Nothing would come out! Finally I muttered an order, some random drink, and slowly pulled forward to the window.

She was there, waiting for me. "Oh! Hey, Juan!"

Another shock. *She knows my name?* I couldn't tell if the urge to throw up came from elation or nervousness. I managed a response, saying "yeah" and giving some strange head nod. I continued to sit in my car, waiting for my drink, completely mortified by my inability to speak. Once she handed me the drink, she said in a perfectly friendly tone, "Have a nice day!"

And how did I respond?

"Yeah . . . totally."

I drove off feeling like a complete idiot. But—*she knew my name.* So, I did the next logical thing. I got a job at the same coffee shop.

Our first weekend shift together, we were finally starting to make small talk, and as we talked I went to blend a drink. Too late I realized my mistake: I hit "start," and the lid-less blender shot sugary drink mix all over me, Brittany, and the customer across the counter.

I was fired on the spot.

But now that I'd had a real conversation with her, we were practically married. So, the next logical thing to do was ask her on a date . . . and she actually said yes. I couldn't believe I was finally about to date my future wife. We went on the date, and I was floating on cloud nine as I walked next to her.

But then she hit me with the four words no one ever wants to hear: "We should be friends."

———

REJECTION *SUCKS.* BIG-TIME. And the reason we all know it sucks is that we've all experienced it.

I hope you've never created an accidental smoothie volcano, but I'd bet that you've been rejected—by someone you have a crush on, a friend, a school, a client, or maybe even a family member.

In the last chapter, we talked about how to have more courage. Namely, you change your story, become the hero, and if (when!) you do fail, you tell yourself, "I'm not there, *yet.*"

That will help you evolve, bit by bit, into a person who has the courage to move into the next phase of the confidence cycle—action.

So, a quick refresher: Energy is that spark that gets you excited about your future *now.* Energy helps you get up the courage to take a couple of steps and cross the bridge toward action. Think of any great classic movie. In *The Princess Bride,* for example, the hero battles something in every major scene. Westley sails through eel-infested waters, climbs a sheer rock face, defeats Inigo, fights Fezzik, outwits Vizzini, trudges through the Fire Swamp, escapes the torture chamber, and bluffs the prince. He's fighting a large-scale battle to win back the princess ... but he's fighting micro-battles each step of the way.

Our journey to building confidence is a lot like that. You, the hero, are trying to win back your confidence. You've fought off the energy killers and reframed your failures, and now it's time to fight your next opponents. As you cross the bridge from energy to action, three opponents pop up, hoping they'll scare you into turning back. But they, too, can be defeated. These opponents represent the three main fears that stand in the way of becoming more confident, and I'm going to introduce you to them in this chapter. Or maybe I should say that I'm going to *re*introduce you. You've probably already met them.

COURAGEOUS PEOPLE SPEND
MORE TIME WITH FEAR

A PEPPERDINE UNIVERSITY study showed that fear and courage can exist—get this—*simultaneously.*[1]

Maybe that makes perfect sense to you. *Duh,* you're thinking. Or maybe you're like me and your thoughts are more like, *No freaking way.*

Let's go back to a few of the stories we've discussed. Ed Sheeran in chapter 1, for instance. Remember, some have suggested he has social anxiety, and yet he's a musical sensation who performs in front of thousands.

In the last chapter, I told you about my brush with sharks. I'm not a brave soul like my wife, Gaby. I hated every minute of that experience (except getting out of the water). But I still did it.

In modern society we have this odd tendency to dismiss those who are good at something, because they're good at it. We watch a speaker bring thousands of people to their feet in roaring applause, and we yawn. We see artists effortlessly bring a blank canvas to life, something we could never do, and we keep walking. We watch some crazy double-back-triple-something at the Olympics, and we scoff, "Yeah, but they're gymnasts."

And we do the same thing with courageous people: "No wonder they acted so heroically; they're courageous." "*I* could never speak up like that. I'm not bold."

Whether we think it consciously or not, we sort of have this notion that courageous people are fearless. Even ChatGPT put "fearless" in a list of ten synonyms for "courageous."

But nothing could be further from the truth. That would

be like saying Simone Biles doesn't have to deal with gravity. Of *course* all the same rules that apply to me and you apply to Biles. She's just put in the time to be able to work *within* those rules. She didn't wake up one day, conquer gravity, then move on with her life. Instead, she's learned to work *with* the laws of science, allowing gravity and gymnastics to coexist. (Kind of like the study showing that courage and fear can coexist.)

I have a friend who was once overwhelmed by numerous fears but grew tired of letting fear run the show. So, she decided to do something about it. She made a list of all of the things that scared her—including helicopters, needles, and singing in front of people—and she decided to check one thing off that list every month. She asked a friend to take a helicopter ride with her. Check. At her doctor's recommendation, she said yes to getting vitamin B12 injections every month. She went to an audition where she was required to sing in front of a panel of casting agents. Each month when it was time to tackle another fear, she was terrified, but she did it anyway. We need to do the same with some of the biggest fears that stand in the way of becoming confident. We need to realize that some fears are like gravity—they aren't going anywhere. It would be nice if they did, but in reality, they're like Uncle René: We all have that uncle. He's going to show up unannounced, and we're all going to know what to do and how to relate to him. So, we've got to get to know those fears well and learn to navigate them.

We see courageous people as special or more capable. In reality, courageous people are just more acquainted with fear than you are. They're almost friendly with fear, hanging out with it on a regular basis, whereas you may only give it a passing nod each time you encounter it. When you choose courage, you don't say goodbye to fear; you are accepting that fear is along for the ride. It's like skydiving, in that you jump out, face what's scary, and relax. In fact, what could kill you—your altitude and the velocity at which you're falling toward the ground—are also the very things that force your parachute to open. A skilled skydiver doesn't flail around. They see the ground, feel the wind, notice the clouds, and think, *Cool. Nice to see you again.*

Just like failure, practice with the opponents is how you're going to get better at working with them (and with Uncle René).

Allow me to introduce you to Uncle René—I mean, the three opponents:

1. Fear of rejection
   > *"If I ask them out, they'll just say no, so I'll save myself the embarrassment."*
   > *"If I apply to the job, I probably won't get chosen, so why bother?"*
   > *"If I share my idea, everyone will probably think it's stupid."*
   > *"If I ask for help, they'll think I'm incompetent."*
2. Fear of the unknown
   > *"What if I take this opportunity and it leads to more stress?"*
   > *"What if I move to a new city and end up lonely?"*
   > *"What if I invest and then the market crashes?"*
   > *"What if I quit my job and can't find another one?"*
3. Fear of inadequacy
   > *"I'm not smart enough to discuss this topic."*
   > *"I don't think I'm good enough for that role."*

> *"I'm not creative enough to come up with a*
> *good idea."*
> *"I'm not experienced enough to take on that*
> *responsibility."*

So, that's the introduction. Now, let's get to know these three fears a little more intimately.

1. FEAR OF REJECTION

MEET EMILY. SHE'S terrified to ask for a raise, convinced that her request will be rejected. The thought of confronting her boss and possibly being told no feels insurmountable. So, she doesn't ask. Eventually, she starts resenting her job and being asked to do additional work she's not being paid to do. She quits and goes back to her old job, where she makes even less money.

I get it. I've been there. Rejection is one of the most painful experiences in life. After my first major crush in high school friend-zoned me on our one and only date, I went into self-preservation mode. I didn't talk, engage, or laugh—my friends dragged me through school as I let the weight of her rejection physically and emotionally crush me. That feeling of rejection was so strong, I convinced myself that it would never end; I just knew I'd lost my wife, *forever.*

Was I a bit dramatic? Yeah, sure. But at some level, rejection is painful.

A study that appeared in an international public health journal concluded that "the phenomenon of belonging and connectedness is universal and appears to be a basic human need in the context of well-being and participation, regardless of the type of community one belongs to."[2] My translation: *Rejection sucks.*

So, how do we navigate this fear?

Eighty Percent Is Up to You

WHEN WE'RE REJECTED, we can focus on all the things we *can't* change—that rejection *will* happen, and that it *will* suck. Or we can focus on the thing we *can* change. So, that's what we do.

Most of us have a deep need to be liked by everyone. But the truth is that some people will *not* like you. Let me say that once more: Some people will simply not like you. They won't like the way you sound, your hair, your overall demeanor, whatever. And there's nothing you can do to change that.

Inspiring news, right?

Well, it's the truth. Most of us have this false expectation that everyone is supposed to like us, and this mentality deters our ability to remain confident. Because whenever someone doesn't, we feel as if we're doing something wrong. But that's not what it means when someone doesn't like us. It just means who we are is wrong for them, and that's OK.

Instead of living your life so that everyone likes you, here's a helpful framework from my friend Josh, one that I've followed for some time now:

Ten percent of people will like you no matter what.

Ten percent of people will *not* like you no matter what.

Eighty percent is up to you.

Too often, we try to change the opinion of the Negative Nancys in our life. (If your name is Nancy, sorry! You're still great!) We suddenly hear the 10 percent who don't like us (and who probably never will), and we spend the bulk of our energy trying to make *those* people like us. All the while, we've ignored everyone else, and by ignoring them, we're losing the 80 percent of people who could be added into our sphere of influence.

What if we gave energy to the people who do have the potential to like us instead of feeling defeated by the 10 percent who don't? What if we ignored the 10 percent who don't like us and intentionally direct our energy toward those who will build us up? The 10 percent who don't like us will always be there. Let's not give them more energy than they deserve.

Remember: Eighty percent is up to you. Focus on them, not the Negative Nancys.

———

LET'S GET BACK to Emily.

Emily was terrified of asking for a raise, convinced that her request would be rejected. The thought of confronting her boss and possibly being told no felt like an insurmountable obstacle. Despite this fear, she decided to focus on what she could control—her own value and confidence. She spent months honing her skills, taking on extra projects, and consistently exceeding expectations. With her newfound confidence and a solid track record to back her up, Emily finally approached her boss. To her surprise, not only was her request for a raise granted, but she was also offered a new leadership role within the company.

2. FEAR OF THE UNKNOWN

SARAH WAS PARALYZED by the fear of moving to a new city, uncertain of what life would be like far from her comfort zone. The thought of starting over in a place where she knew no one felt overwhelming. So, she stayed where she was. She got a job at a local restaurant and always wondered how her life would have been different if she'd taken the leap.

After years of feeling stuck, she finally reached a tipping point. After seeing friends, colleagues, and family members take bold steps in their own lives, she felt like it was a sign to do the same for herself. Seeing her life pass by, haunted by the question "What if?," she decided to take the leap. So, she applied to jobs in New York City, far from her Colorado roots. To her surprise, she got a great job! She packed up her things and booked a one-way ticket.

She started researching neighborhoods, joining online communities, and setting personal goals for her new life. With each courageous choice, her confidence grew. When she finally made the move, not only did she adapt quickly, but she also realized she now had a completely different relationship with the unknown. See, Sarah found out something many of us take years to learn—that it isn't about waiting to have all the answers. Rather, it's about accepting we won't always have those answers, and moving forward regardless of the fear.

———

A FEW YEARS BACK, I was on a flight from San Jose to Las Vegas. As I boarded the plane, I heard over the intercom, "Ladies and gentlemen, welcome to the plane." Not "Thanks for flying American Airlines" or even "I'm Cristina, and your pilot is Eric." She said, "Welcome to the plane." *OK, that's a bit odd.*

I found my seat, put up my luggage, and put my phone into airplane mode. Business as usual. But then—turbulence. Not the if-this-were-my-first-time-flying-I'd-be-scared type of turbulence. I'm telling you, the business travelers in first class who had, like, millions of miles on their accounts were grasping their seats and praying to gods I've never even heard of. Meanwhile, I was white-knuckling on the armrests, thinking, *What's worse? This or sharks?*

I looked for the flight attendant, needing to feel reassured everything was going to be fine. It's a test I always use to know the truth of any situation on an aircraft: *If the flight attendant is calm, we're going to be OK.*

She wasn't calm.

Wait, is she *praying?* I noticed a rosary shaking in her hands as she sat hunched over in her jump seat, eyes shut. *Oh, no. She's got the rosary. She's praying. That's not a good sign. I forgot mine, and this is it. We're finished. The plane's going down.*

Within seconds, I was running through my usual what-to-do-when-I'm-about-to-die checklist. One, call Gaby. Two, call my mom. Three, think of something to say. (Of course, we landed just fine.)

And that's sort of what we all do with fear of the unknown, isn't it? Rarely do we end up guessing that the best will happen; we always assume the worst. Think about it: Someone doesn't come home on time, and we immediately jump to *They died. Their engine blew out. Their ex-girlfriend called and they're back together.* Something ridiculous like that. Yet we *never* think of the implausibly positive outcome. I mean, could they have won the lottery? Gotten offered a hundred grand to go on *The Amazing Race*? Been signed by a modeling agency?

Our fears of the unknown always take us to the extreme—and it's never a good extreme!

The problem with these fears isn't when we spend half or more of a flight going over what-if scenarios. It's how we allow those fears to impact our decision-making with finances, friends, goals, careers, or our dreams.

Job interview? *I'm probably not going to get the job.* Blind date? *We probably won't be compatible.* Dinner with the in-laws? *I'll probably unknowingly say something offensive.*

While often we have evidence of these bad scenarios—we've lost a job, had a blind date, or had a bad dinner or two (probably with Uncle René)—is using past experiences to determine your energy level in future endeavors really a great way to live?

Humans Are Really Bad at Predicting

THE STOCK MARKET is always fluctuating. We all know, in fact, that it's going to go into recession every few decades. It's documented. Yet every time there's a big plummet, lots of people pull their funds out of their 401(k) accounts. The irony here is that the biggest jumps almost always come after these huge dips. So what these people are doing is pulling their money out when their investment is worth the least. As a result, they miss all the big gains as the market shoots up. Once the stock market is back up, they feel safe and buy again. The result isn't that people are "as good as chance" at investing. Amateur investors (which is probably you and definitely me) actually have *much worse* results than you'd get by randomly throwing darts at a dartboard and using that to decide when to sell and when to buy. That's why Warren Buffett says that people's predictions are "worse than useless."[3]

When it comes to investing money in the stock market, we often base decisions on events we just read about. Massive drop? Pull out all your money, save what capital you can. Sudden spike? Pile your money back in and cross your fingers.

But when you look at data going back to 1930, you see that if an investor missed the S&P 500's ten best days each decade, their total return would stand at 28 percent. If, on the other hand, the investor held steady through the ups and downs, their return would have been 17,715 percent.[4]

Our energy is like investing in stocks. When we fail, whether it's a rejection, a missed opportunity, or a breakup, it can be so easy to let our heightened emotions or panic decide our next move. These hits to our energy feel like they're derailing whatever progress we've made so far. All the effort we've been putting in feels like it becomes meaningless when we're faced with the intimidating prospect of starting again. But if you let all of your energy drain away after a big defeat (pulling out every last bit of your money when the stock market drops), not only will your return on confidence be significantly lower, but you'll miss out on the best potential days for gaining that energy back. If the biggest opportunity to make maximum returns is in the days following the loss, then after an unexpected failure, with emotions heightened and heart thumping, choose wisely how you'll respond. Will you back down for fear of losing again? Will you choose to not get back up because it feels too hard? Or will you use that concentrated energy to kick-start your next step toward success?

Just like it "never makes sense to invest in a company's past performance," it doesn't make sense to base your energy off your previous failures.[5] Rather, invest in the market (your energy) when it's down. Invest when you're afraid, when you think it's going to crash, when you think you're about to get rejected. These moments are likely when you'll see your biggest returns.

That's why the advice from professional, long-term financial advisers is for most people to simply "set it and forget it"; they know that if you put your money in the stock market via an index fund, over time you'll make about 10 percent returns, compounded yearly, and that will be enough for you to retire.

Same thing is true for sales professionals—while it varies by industry, many of them have a "close rate" around 20 percent (which means that for every four people who tell them no, one will say yes).

All of this data helps defuse the unknown and offers some general strategies for dealing with uncertainty. Here are my three keys for becoming better friends with the fear of the unknown.

Key 1: Don't Predict, Strategize

TREAT YOUR EMOTIONAL investments into the unknown like a stock market strategy: For sure, your stocks will go down at some point. But the strategy, one proven time and time again, is that *overall,* your money will make more money.

Similarly with artists who are auditioning: Almost always (at least 99 percent of the time), they're getting rejected. But they don't react to any of these. It's just part of the process. They don't view their job as performing in shows; they view it as going to auditions. Getting to actually perform is just a cherry on top.

Whatever your courageous move is, don't try to predict what's going to happen next (you can't). Just pick a strategy based on logic, or based on industry standards, and stick to your plan.

Let's say that you're trying to open a coffee shop. You could go with your gut and just make decisions as they pop up—on your good days you'll think you're going to turn a fantastic profit, and on your bad days you'll wonder, *Why did I even do this?* Instead, though, you could use industry information to understand seasonal changes in your business, and this will help you weather the highs and lows of entrepreneurship.

If you're preparing for a presentation, instead of trying to predict how the audience will receive your content, focus on the core components of a great presentation. Work on your body language, opening story, and key takeaways. When you do, the audience will resonate with your talk.

When you're talking to potential clients, it can be easy to profile them into categories, such as "qualified buyers" or "unqualified buyers." This creates assumptions that may or may not be true and can lead to disappointment. Instead, work on gaining a deep understanding of each client's needs, their goals, and how you can align with those goals. They'll feel more valued, and you'll be more likely to close the deal.

Key 2: Know the Numbers

DEPENDING ON WHAT you're trying to deal with, the numbers can help calm your nerves. For instance, it was a little ridiculous for me to get nervous about that plane encountering turbulence. These are the chances of that plane going down: 0.00000001 percent.[6]

What are you planning on handling? Do you know the numbers? If you do, often it can shine some light onto the reality of the situation. Even if the numbers *aren't* in your favor, that knowledge helps you.

One of the reasons salespeople don't get upset is that they *already know* they're going to fail *most* of the time. *Most* people will reject them. *Most* people will not answer the phone.

If you're trying to get into Harvard, knowing that *most likely* you aren't going to get in is actually helpful. It doesn't mean you shouldn't try. Not at all. It just means that knowing that Harvard's acceptance rate is low will help you deal with rejection and make alternative plans. I know people who went to Harvard, who became Olympians, who became a Navy SEAL, or any one of a number of crazy things. All of them knew their chances of success, and in fact they had learned to have a good relationship with the fear of the unknown.

Here's how this applies to your confidence. Say that you're trying to be more confident in relationships, so you decide to ask a few people out. Guess what? The goal isn't to have a bunch of significant others; rather, at least for most of us, the goal is to find *one* right person, which means most romantic relationships won't work out. They fail at many different points:

- You could ask someone out and they may tell you no.
- They may say no to a second date.
- They may break up with you.

That's all a reality, but once you realize you are looking not to be a relationship expert but to be an expert at just one person, you realize that most people aren't a good match.

Say that you're a new researcher who's trying to get your paper accepted. You can start submitting your findings to journals, knowing that you'll probably get mostly nos. You're only looking for one journal to say yes to you. Framing this inside your head from the beginning will allow your confidence to stay intact as you receive a bunch of rejection letters.

The same goes for job applications, scholarships, book proposals, auditions, and even promotions. Generally speaking, the answer is going to be no. Once you understand that most of the time you'll be "losing," you'll feel much better about wading through those losses.

No one gets this more than people who go to professional performing auditions: They remember that it only takes one yes to land that starring role!

Key 3: Let Losses Go Quickly

WHEN YOU UNDERSTAND the game you're playing and you're sticking to a strategy, you're able to let go of failures quickly.

Roger Federer once explained this. Even if you don't know that much about tennis, you've probably heard about Federer, as he was one of the greatest men's tennis players of all time. You're probably not surprised to learn that he won 80 percent of the matches he played. But get this—he won only *54 percent* of the points within those matches. While that may sound statistically impossible, it makes sense because of the way tennis is scored. But that's not really the point.[*]

Federer knew that he didn't need to win every point. In fact, he barely needed to win more than half. But—and this is

---

[*]　Sorry. I had to.

critical—if he was going to be losing points 46 percent of the time, he needed to have some thick skin and quickly let things go. If he'd gotten upset about every point he lost, he never would have become the champion he was.

3. FEAR OF INADEQUACY

MARK WAS NERVOUS about attending a holiday party where he knew only a few people, fearing that he wasn't interesting or smart enough to contribute to conversations with strangers. The thought of mingling in a room full of highly intelligent people made him feel inadequate and out of place.

Have you ever felt that way before, lacking the confidence to even say hello? Growing up as an overweight kid was not easy. Though I tried to be happy around friends, my life was based on fake confidence as fragile as a bubble that could be popped by a single negative comment. In fact, it *was* popped, on several occasions, by my dad. Unlike my mother, who filled me up with endless encouragement, my father was incapable of approving of anything I did. If I hammered a nail into the wall, he would hammer it one more time. If I moved something on the table, he would move it just a bit more. His constant adjustments reminded me every day that he expected perfection and that I was incapable of providing it. This inability to live up to his expectations began to shape how I viewed myself, eventually becoming the reason I stopped caring about my weight. I was never enough for him, and over time I convinced myself I wasn't enough for anyone.

Because I believed this lie, I then allowed myself to buy into society's too-simple notion that "no matter what you do, you are enough." While this felt good in contrast to my dad's harsh judgment, it stalled my growth, just in a different way. (True, I may be *enough,* but that doesn't mean I can't grow, right?) My father's constant revisions told me that no matter how much I tried to improve, I would never be good enough, yet society's abounding approval didn't push me to improve at all. Instead, I grew stagnant; I became complacent.

When I was a kid, my teachers used to always say, "Focus on your strengths." Now I think, *What a terrible idea!* Not only does neglecting your weaknesses lead to less overall growth, but it forces you away from a choice you have every right to make. Weaknesses are just potential strengths in need of some confidence, just more opportunities to excel—not a defining characteristic dooming you to be one way. You are not a fixed person, with limited abilities; improvement is always an option.

I was told that my speech abilities were a weakness. If I had listened to my teachers, I never would have discovered my career. Now, public speaking is one of my greatest strengths because I chose for it to be. I didn't let that voice telling me "You're not enough" compel me to give up. I let each failure propel me forward, reassuring myself that with every failure, I improved that much more.

A Study of Elite Swimmers

IN THE 1980S, Daniel Chambliss studied elite swimmers, both Olympians and world-record holders, to understand what makes a champion.

Interestingly, what Chambliss discovered made him believe there is essentially *no such thing as talent.* Instead, he said that the entire pursuit of elite swimming came down to a few small things:[7]

1. How often someone practiced
2. Focus on small improvements
3. Constantly challenging themselves

The amount of practice goes without saying—but I think a lot of people discount the other two habits.

What Chambliss discovered was that most swimmers (and people) focus on the big days—the days when they set a record, get a promotion, and so on—but the champions, the ones who ended up as elites in their field, celebrated small wins, often focusing on the smallest of improvements to a specific area.

Lastly, the elite swimmers were constantly challenging themselves with new coaches, leagues, and pools. They didn't dominate a league and stay there. And that's tough—it's one thing to pick yourself up from failure, but giving up a league that you're *crushing*? Nearly impossible. But Olympic swimmers who want to perform at their best developed a habit of constant challenges. They would constantly move up to another league, or set micro-goals on the daily of shaving off just another tenth or hundredth of a second.

So, for us, here's how we can tackle the fear of inadequacy.

Stop Worrying About "Talent"

THIS IS GOING to sound backward to our Western minds, because we just love the idea of a young, talented hotshot. But listen to what Chambliss said about talent:

Most Olympic champions, when their history is studied, seem to have overcome sharp adversity in their pursuit of success. Automobile accidents, shin splints, twisted ankles, shoulder surgery are common in such tales. In fact, they are common in life generally. While some necessary minimum of physical strength, heart/lung capacity, or nerve density may well be required for athletic achievement (again, I am not denying differential advantages), that minimum seems both difficult to define and markedly low, at least in many cases. Perhaps *the crucial factor is not natural ability at all, but the willingness to overcome natural or unnatural disabilities* of the sort that most of us face, ranging from minor inconveniences in getting up and going to work, to accidents and injuries, to gross physical impairments. And if *the basic level of talent needed, then, seems so low as to be nearly universally available,* perhaps the very concept of talent itself—no longer differentiating among performers—is better discarded altogether.[8]

I'll sum it up: After conducting one of the most famous studies of elite athletes in the world, Chambliss doesn't believe in talent. In fact, his paper is titled "The Mundanity of Excellence." In a way, he made excellence, even at the Olympic level, simply a byproduct of the correct ingredients. He showed that it's a mixture of doing the right things in the right amounts with the right mentality, and when these ingredients are present, the outcomes are predictable, as they are when baking a cake. There is no secret sauce, even for an Olympic athlete.

We've got to learn to stare down our feelings of inadequacy and realize that we all have about the same level of "adequacy," whatever that even means. If we want to be better at something, we can choose to put in the work, and we will get better. It's that simple.

Go Crazy for a 1 Percent Improvement

IN HIS STUDY, Chambliss noted how the best of the best always found an area to improve in. This is also true with some of the best live performers in the arts. A performer I know talked about noticing the difference between fellow performers who were incredible and those who were merely good. The incredible performers weren't the pretty ones, the ones with the most "talent," the ones who started out the best, or the ones with the most professional training. Rather, all of the best performers had one thing in common—they'd pick one area and go nuts if they improved it: "I finally nailed that half turn!" "I tried something new with the inflection on one of my lines, and it worked!" People who were doing the same show over and over again often would get bored, but not the elite ones—it was like they *enjoyed* the half tweaks, the barely noticeable changes. Over time, those micro-improvements led to dramatic differences in outcome. That's kind of like the whole message of this book!

———

SO, WHAT HAPPENED to Mark, who was nervous about going to a holiday party where he didn't know many people?

Despite his fear, Mark decided to focus on what he could control—being genuinely curious and open in his interactions. He took a deep breath and started sparking conversations with new people. To his surprise, not only were people interested in what he had to say, but they also appreciated his unique perspective. This experience boosted his confidence and showed him that he had more to offer than he initially believed. And that encouraged him to continue building his social skills.

MAKING FRIENDS

ONCE WE MAKE friends with our opponents that everyone's scared of, they don't seem so scary anymore. If you can unmask the fears, shine some light on what's bothering you, and find ways to include those fears in your life—because they really aren't going anywhere anyway—you'll learn that it's OK to have fear and courage *at the same time.*

Without opponents blocking your path, you'll be able to continue your revolution around the Confidence Cycle, and you'll be ready for the next step . . . action.

Confidence Cheat Sheet

- Courageous people aren't fearless. They just have a better relationship with their fears.
- There are three key fears that you've got to get to know and start interacting with on better terms:
  1. Fear of rejection
  2. Fear of the unknown
  3. Fear of inadequacy
- In his famous paper "The Mundanity of Excellence," Daniel Chambliss wrote about a number of factors that produce

the world's most elite athletes, and what he found is that those factors have almost nothing to do with talent.

- Those who, in the long run, become the most successful in any given area are those who celebrate the 1 percent improvements.

Micro-Step

Everyone struggles with the fear of the unknown, and often this one is linked to the other two fears (rejection and inadequacy). So, let's defuse that fear right now.

1. What's one thing you've been considering doing but have been too scared to tackle? It could be asking some guy out on a date, starting a business, or starting a neighborhood movie night. Whatever it is, write it down.

2. Research what's most likely to happen, and the associated chances: "If I start a business, most likely I'll make no money the first two years, and then it will turn profitable."

3. Make a decision on your next move based on the data.

Micro-Action

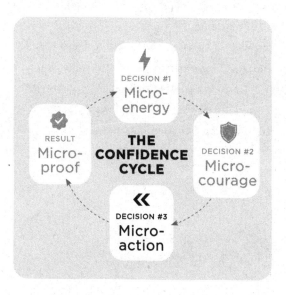

MICRO-ACTION: *Completing a small action and accepting it as proof of capability.*

So, you've generated some energy and built up some courage, and now you're ready for action. But before you take a giant leap into something like moving across the country, quitting your job to start a business, or signing up for *American Idol,* I'm going to teach you how to break those bigger goals into tiny little steps that you can tackle. We'll call these tiny steps micro-actions. Basically, this means you complete a small action and accept it as proof of capability, regardless of whether you "succeeded" or felt scared during the process. Taking the step is action enough, regardless of outcome.

In the next chapter, you're going to learn how to break down those big confidence goals into tinier steps. And in chapter 8, I provide a list of baby steps you can use to get started on some of the most-requested confidence items, like getting in shape or changing careers.

7.

Baby Steps Only

———

BET YOU'VE HEARD OF DAVID AND GOLIATH—THE ORIGINAL underdog story. If you don't remember your Sunday school lesson, let me remind you: The little teenage shepherd David takes on the biggest, baddest warrior around, Goliath, and comes out on top.

We all love that story, because we all have a desire to be David—taking on the giants in our lives.

But there's another part of that story that always seems to get missed. You see, when David volunteered to take on Goliath, no one believed he could do it—understandably. He had to convince them he was up to the task. According to the legend, David doesn't try to convince his comrades that he's the man for the job by showing off his (nonexistent) military skills or telling them how good he is with a slingshot. Instead, he tells the king and the other soldiers about smaller actions he'd taken already. Namely, that he'd killed other, smaller creatures, and he'd just be increasing the trophy size when he took on Goliath.

David said, "I've been a shepherd, tending sheep for my father. Whenever a lion or bear came and took a lamb from the flock, I'd go after it, knock it down, and rescue the lamb. If it turned on me, I'd grab it by the throat, wring its neck, and kill it. Lion or bear, it made no difference—I killed it. And I'll do the same to this Philistine pig."[1]

You notice that? He gives a progression, a series of small steps from one action to the next: He was an everyday shepherd, learned how to kill a lion and a bear, and now he's ready to take on an even bigger enemy.

But we all somehow miss *that* part of the story. We just want to tackle the giants.

THE HERO'S JOURNEY

IN 1949, WRITER and professor Joseph Campbell put forth the notion that nearly all mythological literature is based on a single structure, called the "monomyth" or, most commonly, the hero's journey.[2] His theory contains seventeen named stages, but they're broken down into three broad phases:

SEPARATION: The hero is called to adventure and must accept or reject this call.

INITIATION: The hero has reached the point of no return, encountering a series of trials or challenges that must be overcome. The hero must continue on or fail.

RETURN: The hero comes back from adventure altered, with new skills and a new identity.

You catch the word "series"? Hmm ... Sounds interesting, doesn't it? Like, maybe you don't get to battle the main boss on level ten without knocking out some little devils earlier.

This structure, adopted by countless books, movies, TV shows, and comic books, continues to be the primary narrative we think of in storytelling. Have you seen the movie *Aladdin*? Most likely you have, either as a kid or with your own kids. To refresh your memory, Aladdin is a homeless, orphaned street thief who cleverly comes into possession of a magical lamp. He rubs the lamp and out pops Genie, ready to grant Aladdin three wishes. Aladdin's first wish is to be a prince, for the girl he loves, Princess Jasmine, can only marry a prince. His second wish is to be saved from drowning. And the third? Well, that's a plot spoiler, so I'm not telling.

Let's take a deeper look at the major plot points here. When we first meet Aladdin, his life is a bit hopeless and he doesn't think he'll ever make it out of his poor situation. However, his heart is good—he's humble and has the desire to help others. Then he meets the Genie, and things start looking up. In one sense, his life is getting better—when he's pretending to be a prince he's got access to nicer clothes, plenty of money, more power, and the princess. But his heart hardens a bit and he becomes more self-focused.

In the middle of the story Aladdin becomes even more selfish, his callousness beginning to affect his relationships with those around him. Not to mention that the villain, Jafar, and his parrot sidekick, Iago, are trying to get rid of Aladdin. Things are pretty bad. In fact, they're much worse than when we first meet Aladdin in the beginning of the story. Then, in the very next beat, Aladdin conquers Jafar, and simultaneously

he overcomes his selfish tendencies, using his last wish to—
Oh, right, I'm not going to spoil it for you.

In other words, up until the moment Aladdin succeeds,
he's going through the worst time of his life. It's absolutely
inconceivable to skip this part of the hero's journey when writing a book or movie, as it's what makes the story good. It also
heightens the stakes. So, why should we skip this part in our
own lives? All the little steps it takes to actually accomplish
what we're striving for just make our story greater.

PERFECTIONISM IS THE
ENEMY OF PROGRESS

I'VE TOLD YOU about my dad's compulsive habit of fixing everything I did. His standard was perfection in *everything*. If I
screwed something in, he would check whether it was tight.
There wasn't a *single time* in my entire life with him that felt as
though I did something right.

My dad, who grew up in the middle of a war in Nicaragua,
was raised in a purely machismo culture. He was an amazing
father in many ways. He was supportive, caring, and fully
present in our lives, and he always wanted what was best for
my brother, sister, and me. But his perfectionism often got the
better of him, and I was often the one on the other end of his
high standards. He'd always say, "It needs to be perfect. If
you're not going to do it perfectly, don't even bother."

For years I tried to achieve this elusive target. I bent over
backward to learn his preferences, to make sure everything I
did for him was just right—but the target I was aiming for
didn't even exist. We'd do projects around the house, and what
I did was never enough. I was putting pressure on myself to do

what was impossible. Eventually, after endless frustrating attempts to be perfect, I gave up. I chose to stop trying and accept that I was an embarrassment to the family, a fat, incapable kid who couldn't do anything right. If I couldn't be perfect, there was no use in trying at all.

When we give ourselves just two choices—perfection or nothing—many of us will choose the latter. I did.

As we touched on in chapter 5, we live in a society of extremes:

- "Eat kale, or don't bother with nutrition."
- "Become an Iron Man triathlete, or let your weight go."
- "Become a millionaire, or keep your boring day job."
- "Live your dreams, or become a stoic."

When given these options, we end up in one of two places—either we choose to let it all go, or we fight for as long as we can for perfection and *then* let it all go. However you look at it, I am not eating the kale.

And that's what we all do, every day, when we want to achieve everything we dream of, and achieve it right now. At the same time, we feel like if we don't achieve it immediately, we have no choice but to fall off completely.

Often we sabotage our journey toward confidence by choosing targets that are so unattainable, sometimes even invisible, that every attempt is doomed to end in failure. We mistake these targets for high standards. So, while we are aiming for the "highest possible standard," we are ensuring our lowest possible self-confidence. We need to change the narrative. We must set the *right* expectations for our confidence.

Maybe you're not confident enough to ask for the promotion right now. That's OK. What about just speaking up and asking for that one Friday off you've been wanting so that you can spend a three-day weekend in Vegas?

Maybe you aren't ready to burn the ship, quit your job, and dive headfirst into your own business. Why not try shrinking your goal, making it smaller? Try starting a blog about your business or taking a course on the industry you'd want to build in.

Frequently we fail to get started because we've set our sights on a task that feels too daunting.

There are a lot of ways to stall our confidence journey. But just as we've been looking for micro-energy and micro-courage, it's time to start taking micro-action. Earlier, we defined micro-action as completing a small action and accepting it as proof of capability, regardless of whether we "succeeded" or felt scared during the process. Completion is proof of capability.

Researcher James L. Mandigo studied how to enhance motivation through optimal challenges and found that the right-size challenge is the one that's most likely to produce the confidence we seek:

> When individuals are successful at an optimally challenging activity (i.e., not too easy, not too hard), their competence is enhanced . . . [and they] are more likely to have a quality subjective experience and be intrinsically motivated to take part in the activity. . . . However, if exposed to continuous imbalances (i.e., skill does not equal challenge), participants can become frustrated or bored, which may eventually lead to their withdrawal from the activity.[3]

If the task is too easy, we'll get bored, and no skill will be gained. On the other hand, if the task is too hard, we'll become frustrated.

In relationships, we don't want an overly critical partner (or one who doesn't help us improve). We want one who will encourage us on our way to progress. If my dad had balanced his expectation with positive feedback, maybe I wouldn't have struggled to the point of giving up entirely. I wish I could go back and tell young Juan that imperfect action is a thousand times better than no action at all.

Here's a quick trick: Put a date on it. That's right—whatever that big goal you have is, break it down into the *smallest possible action* you can take, the most micro of baby steps. Do you want to start a business? Making your first dollar is a great first step. Do you want to be a public speaker? Giving a five-minute speech over FaceTime to your loved ones is an easy move. Do you want to have the confidence to tell your kids no? Practicing a role-play where you say no could be the first step for you.

So, now that you have it broken down and have identified a first baby step, *put it on the calendar.* That's right, schedule it, even if the baby step takes only five minutes. That way, you've broken it down even more. You don't have to do it right now; you just need to schedule it. Then, when the time comes, it's already on your calendar.

JUAN BECOMES A RUNNER

FOR A LONG time, as I said earlier, I would get a sharp pain in my right side whenever I ran. I talked to a few doctors—professionals who are experts on pain—and they told me that when I run, I should pause whenever I feel pain and wait until the pain goes away, and then I could continue running. So for years that's what I did. Whenever I ran, I'd start out great; then, at about 100 or maybe 150 yards, I'd feel a punch of pain in my right side. I'd stop, wait a few minutes, then continue on when I felt comfortable. After all, that's what the experts told me to do. Plus, it just made sense: Pain is no good, so I did my best to avoid it. I'd also tell myself that I was certainly avoiding a bigger problem. Who knew what could happen if I just ran through the pain? (I mean, my insides could explode, right?)

Fast-forward to a few years later. One morning I was sitting on the couch, with my life meter drifting somewhere around "slothful." I wasn't asleep, but honestly, sleep might have been a more productive state. I was bored and lazy, and my prospects for the day weren't great—at that moment, I was getting dangerously close to wasting all the daylight by binge-watching about ten hours of a Netflix show I can't even remember the title of.

Then someone invited me to a barbecue. Maybe I've overdramatized the seriousness of the invitation in that scenario, but to me, my options were:

OPTION 1: Stay home and stare into a square box as it turned me into a zombie.

OPTION 2: Turn off the TV, go see my friends, and save the world (or at least inject some meaning into my day).

Many people can binge-watch a TV show and live to tell the tale, but my ultimate decision to flick it off and go to my friend's house was a big moment. For some reason, I decided not only to go to my friend's house but to *run* there. Now, I hadn't run more than 200 yards straight in my whole life. Ever. Not when

I played soccer as a teenager, not when I "ran" to the grocery store—not even when a burglar was chasing me (which, thankfully, had never happened, because I might have tried to call a time-out every hundred yards or so). But that day, for whatever reason, I decided I was going to run the whole three miles.

Predictably, at about 150 yards, the same old stitch flared up in my right side. By now, after years of training myself to stop the moment that pain appeared, I could hear my brain telling me, *OK, Juan! Time to stop.* But for some reason I can't explain, I just kept running.

The voice got louder: *Ahem—Juan? Feel that pain? It's time to stop!*

But I kept running for another 50 yards.

Juan! Stop. Now!

The voice even reminded me of all the bad things that would certainly happen if I didn't stop running:

- My kidneys would surely explode.
- I'd rupture some deeply important organ I didn't even know existed.
- My body would just inexplicably shut down and refuse to take another step, because I wasn't treating it fairly.

But guess what? I'm writing this, aren't I?

After I spent a few moments fighting the voice, the pain just disappeared, and I began running *pain-free.*

OK, if you're someone who pulls on their Lululemon gear every morning and then hits a daily 5K, getting less than half a mile into a run without buckling under the pressure isn't a big deal. But for me, that was a truly life-changing moment.

My whole life I'd been doing the start-pain-wait routine. I had never imagined that all I needed to do was deal with a little bit of pain for a few seconds, after which the pain would suddenly disappear and then I'd be free!

Three miles later, I made it to my friend's house, *without* any pain in my side.

Don't worry—this book's not about running. I'm not an expert in that department (though I can now go ten miles with no stops and no pain). It's about the process.

You see, even though running to that party was a small victory, it illustrates a perfectly salient point: Messy action is better than no action.

———

YOU KNOW WHAT I love about that story? I didn't show up at my friend's house looking like an Abercrombie and Fitch model. I was sweaty, dirty, and all the rest. My run was far from perfect.

But I got there. And the deal is, you'll never get there if you don't eventually take some action.

Even with all the right energy and courage in the world, at some point you need to make a move. You have to go for it. It doesn't have to be *much,* but you need to do something.

So, let's start, right now, finding a few micro-actions you can take to get moving.

WHAT ARE YOU AFTER?

WHAT IS IT that you're after? "Get more confidence" isn't going to cut it here. Let's really think—what's a more *specific* goal?

Here are a few examples of what I mean:

- Lose forty pounds by the end of this year
- Go back to school before turning thirty-five
- Start a family within the next three years
- Get promoted by the end of the quarter
- Learn another language before that trip next summer

Note the time frame attached to each goal to prevent it from being stagnant. Once you have defined, specifically, what you are moving toward, the next step is to . . . well, take the next *right* step:

- What's one thing you can do to start losing those forty pounds?
- What's one micro-step you can take toward going back to school?
- How can you get something on the calendar to learn that language?

If all you can do is make one ounce of improvement or change 1 percent of your life, then this book has done its job. My goal isn't to dramatically change your life by the end of the chapter. I want you to see the value of small, incremental progress in the pursuit of bigger goals.

And then I want you to *celebrate* those micro-steps!

Scott's Thirty-Minute Walk to Nowhere

GROWING UP, SCOTT was never an athlete. He was a straight-A student, he was president of the student council, and he had great friends. But all of that brainiac-ness came at a price; he'd totally ignored all things physical. His friends and family would always joke about Scott's inability to do anything remotely athletic. If he was asked to go take out the trash, the comment immediately following would be, "Don't hurt yourself! We know that's a lot of cardio for you."

Traditionally, it hadn't bothered Scott. He just stayed in his lane. You could always find him in the library. Even so, Scott looked up to his friends who were athletes, and to others in great shape, and he wanted to unlock that part of his life. But he'd never stepped foot in a gym.

Scott took an incredible baby step to accomplish his goal. He didn't decide to do a short workout, or any workout at all. Instead, he started his get-in-shape journey with nothing more than walking *to* the gym. He decided to walk to the campus gym, then immediately turn around and walk home. It was fifteen minutes each way; at the very least, he'd be getting in a half hour of walking.

You know how much confidence it takes to go into a gym by yourself and stare at machines that you don't know how to use? A *lot*.

But do you know how much confidence it takes to walk to the gym and then turn around? Very little.

One day, as Scott was doing his normal walk-to-the-gym-and-go-home routine, someone coming toward the gym passed him walking away and stopped for a chat.

"Hey! I see you coming out of the gym every day. What's your name?"

Immediately feeling like an imposter, Scott replied, "Yeah, I'm trying to get in shape. Just finding it hard to figure out what to do."

The guy looked at him for a few moments, then said bluntly, "Why don't you come meet me tomorrow and we can do a workout together?" Scott agreed. The next day, they met up and did a workout. To Scott's surprise, it actually wasn't as bad as he thought. Today, Scott is a gym regular.

Look at all the baby steps he took to get there:

MICRO-ACTION 1: Walk to the gym.

MICRO-ACTION 2: Be honest with the stranger about his lack of understanding.

MICRO-ACTION 3: Show up at the gym for a workout with a new friend.

I'm sure Scott didn't plan to make any friends, but he did intentionally take the first micro-action, by deciding to walk to the gym. That action naturally led to someone bumping into him to talk. Then honesty just poured out. At that point the other person knew that Scott needed some help, but it didn't take *that* much from Scott to be honest. Next, his new acquaintance invited him to come for a workout the next day, and it's *so* much easier to go to the gym with someone who knows what they're doing.

All along the way, Scott's confidence was growing. *I walked to the gym. I made a friend. They didn't laugh at me. They invited me somewhere. I did a workout.*

It was the Confidence Cycle playing out in real time!

Celebrate the Small

WHEN A BABY is learning to walk, what is the parents' response when the baby stands for the first time? They jump up and down, they clap and cheer, they tell their baby how strong they are and how amazing their progress is. And what happens when the baby takes their first step? Even more celebration. The parents whip out the camera, ready to capture this monumental achievement.

That first time, the baby takes one step and falls down. The next time, after more clapping and encouragement, the baby manages to take two steps. Finally, by the third time, they make it all the way across the living room to collapse into their parents' open arms.

Everyone knows why it's exciting when a baby learns to walk. An infant's legs are practically made of Jell-O, which makes standing a feat in itself. And when they're old enough to walk, they're old enough to start doing other amazing things like dancing and running. This tiny victory opens the door for a world of possibilities.

But as we grow, "learning to walk" in other areas of life, we forget to celebrate when we take another step. Maybe we reserve our praise for more utilitarian achievements like good grades and sports achievements. Or we set our standard for celebration so high, like graduating from high school or college, that we hardly experience any celebrations at all. And while there's nothing wrong with celebrating these milestone moments, we miss out on all the previous wins that came before them. Celebrating only the big moments is like expecting our confidence to spike once we've achieved a change in identity. Remember, confidence *isn't* found in the big moments; it's developed in the small steps.

For me, one way I "learned to walk" was learning how to be consistent, and celebrating each time I accomplished what I set out to do. Originally, for me, that was simply getting out of bed each morning. Maybe for you it's celebrating each time you get yourself to start a workout, or celebrating your morning five-minute journal routine, or celebrating each time you reach out to one new person.

It's the small, celebrated wins that compound into much larger achievements.

Small Actions No One Sees

CONSIDER FORMER BASKETBALL PLAYER Jay Williams's recollection of his experience playing against Kobe Bryant. The morning before Williams's team, the Chicago Bulls, played Bryant's team, the Los Angeles Lakers, Williams wanted to get a head start, so he decided to go into practice early. When he got to the arena, he found Bryant, drenched in sweat; he had already been practicing for over an hour, and he didn't leave for another half hour after that. No matter where he was, Kobe Bryant was "the first to arrive, and the last to leave. . . . His fulfillment came from pushing daily to reach his full potential."[4]

The Lakers beat the Bulls that night, Bryant having scored forty of the total points.

Do you think Bryant got his name chanted in the stands by millions across the world by focusing on single victories? Do you think he stepped onto that court with a hope and a prayer that he could dunk at the right moments or score when he had the chance? Absolutely not. He worked every day toward his goal, and every night, too, honing his craft, practicing and practicing, until his capabilities supported his confidence. He didn't have to worry about making mistakes in public because he had already made them a hundred times over in private. Kobe found his confidence in the empty gym, not on the court in front of screaming fans.

This isn't me telling you to go to an empty gym at three in the morning to develop confidence. This is me telling you your confidence is found when no one is watching: in your living room, in the middle of the night, early in the morning, or while you study, rehearse your speech, work on your writing, find the perfect outfit, or play your piano. Don't stop at a thousand steps, or even two thousand; in fact, don't stop at any step. Just keep practicing.

Here's how you can use this to build confidence. Let's say you have a thirty-minute presentation that you are slated to give in two months. You can start by breaking down the preparation into twenty-minute practice sessions. The first week, just focus on the first five minutes of the presentation. Once you feel confident about the first five minutes, move on to the next ten minutes. As you learn your content, you'll feel more confident and be ready to rock the stage!

Or let's say you want to build confidence in a new leadership role at work. This may look like taking thirty minutes a day before work starts to learn more about your team and study current projects. Once you feel like you have an understanding of the role, your next micro-action can be to reach out to senior leadership who have been in your position and ask for their mentorship.

None of these actions is earth-shattering in itself, but together they are the building blocks of confidence. Confidence is found in the micro-actions we take when no one is watching.

CONCLUSION

IN 1501, MICHELANGELO was commissioned to carve a statue for the Opera del Duomo and was given a slab of stone known as "The Giant," a massive "unworkable" piece of marble that had been abandoned for forty years after several artists claimed "imperfections in the marble's grain." It had been left to deteriorate in the Florence cathedral, "grown rough after years of exposure to the elements." Yet despite the stone's obvious flaws, Michelangelo accepted the challenge, and with meticulous effort, carved the famous statue *David*.[5]

Do you know at what point an ordinary block of stone becomes a statue? Does that happen when the artist decides the work is complete? Or when another artist remarks, "What a lovely statue"?

With every micro-action, another piece of stone gets carved away. No amount of force will more quickly reveal the sculpture beneath, so give yourself time. You might not feel like Michelangelo's *David* right now, but with enough small strikes, even the roughest stone (the kind of "unworkable" stone that was used to sculpt *David*) can become an eternal symbol of independence and strength.

Notice what Michelangelo did: He didn't go from block to perfection overnight. He made a decision to keep chiseling, to keep going, even when it was uncomfortable—just like I had to do when I was learning to run. We can imagine that much of the time Michelangelo was working alone, without anyone else but him there to celebrate each time he got the nose a little more perfect or the shoulder a little more rounded.

For you, recognize that to reach your confidence goals, you're going to need to be the hero in the story, take messy action, and get started.

In the next chapter, I break down ten common confidence scenarios—from weight loss to parenting—and then give you the exact micro-action you can take to start toward your goals.

Confidence Cheat Sheet

- Too often we fail because we aim too high. Don't worry about slaying the dragon today; you'll get there. First, learn to tackle the little things. Then progress.
- Perfectionism kills progress. Often, we believe that if we can't do something perfectly, we shouldn't start at all. This is a false dichotomy!
- Celebrate small wins—even if they aren't pretty.
- Be willing to take actions that no one else sees.

Micro-Step

I'll make this super easy. First, list your big goal. Then, list the next action you can take to get there. Finally, put it on the calendar!

Three rules to help you take a micro-step toward your big goal:

1. Define your big goal, and put a date on it: *I want to enter the Boston Marathon by 2027.*

2. Choose a micro-action that's not too easy and not too hard: *Buy my running shoes.*

3. Put a date on that micro-action: *Buy my running shoes this weekend.*

I know, none of that may sound like you're getting much closer to the Boston Marathon, but you know what? You haven't read the next chapter, on momentum, which will show you just how powerful these small moves can be when stacked together.

8.

Ten Micro-Actions

———

*Inaction breeds doubt and fear. Action breeds
confidence and courage. If you want to conquer
fear, do not sit home and think about it.
Go out and get busy.*

—DALE CARNEGIE

THIS CHAPTER IS GOING TO BE A LITTLE DIFFERENT. I'VE PUT
together ten micro-actions, any one of which you can take
right now to start tackling whatever area you want to make
strides in with your confidence. From dating to starting your
own business, these actions will jump-start your confidence
cycle.

YOUR BABY STEPS TO
A NEW BEACH BODY

IT TURNS OUT that people in the gym are super-nice people, but
they can feel a little intimidating at first. There's probably
nothing scarier for a new gym-goer than going to a fitness
studio full of gym-heads who know exactly what they're doing
on complicated machinery. In fact, I'd say one of the main
psychological barriers people face when it comes to getting

into shape is that they don't want to show up and look awkward in front of everyone.

So, I have a way you can start building confidence in the gym, right now.

In the last chapter, we talked about Scott, who just walked thirty minutes a day to and from the gym. That works if you're within walking distance. But if you're not, here's an idea.

Show up at the gym and walk on the treadmill for thirty minutes. Ignore *all* the other gym equipment. After you've gone a few times and you get acclimated to walking for half an hour, take a look around (without being too creepy), find *one* machine you want to learn, and watch what everyone does while they're on it. After about a week, you'll know how to do the treadmill *and* use one machine! You can keep this up and just add one or two machines every few days until you have the confidence to ask someone how to use another machine.

MICRO-ACTION: Go to the gym and hop on the treadmill for thirty minutes, keeping a (non-creepy) eye out for one machine that you can try to use next time. Then, when you think you can handle it, move on to that machine. Be willing to fail a couple of times, but as your confidence builds, you'll be able to take breaks between sets. During those breaks, watch *just one more* machine. Keep going until you've got an entire workout plan!

TAKE CONTROL OF YOUR
FINANCES ONE DEBT AT A TIME

BEN IS THIRTY-TWO years old, single, and terrible at saving. The reason? Credit card debt. It started with signing up for a weekend conference that he couldn't quite afford, and it has been snowballing ever since. When it comes to finances, the only compounding you want is on the money you've invested, not the interest on money you owe. He lives in a big city, where everything is quite pricey, and he hangs out with friends who are not as financially constrained as he is. He wants to keep up with everyone around him, so he spends freely and employs the most sophisticated financial strategy available: avoidance. He doesn't look at his credit card statements, refuses to log into online banking unless he absolutely needs to, and practices the hope-things-get-better approach.

One day he was having a conversation with a friend, Drew, who is an entrepreneur, is financially secure with zero debt, and has an investment portfolio worth more than six figures. "Ben, you're thirty-two. When are you going to take your finances seriously?" Drew asked.

Ben took his usual stance: "I'm young! I've got time."

Drew paused, then said, "Listen, I know looking at your finances is scary, but if you don't figure this out, you'll always feel behind." This was officially an intervention.

The thought of looking at his finances was absolutely terrifying, giving Ben the feeling of a pit in his stomach. He knew something needed to change.

After their conversation, Ben logged into his online banking and courageously stared at his financial life. He decided that his first step would be to pay $100 toward one credit card.

By paying off that first $100, he proved to himself that he could take a micro-action, and he realized that if he just did this over and over, he could actually change his situation. Starting to pay off the debt gave him the courage to start saving. And the act of paying off debt gave him the energy to start a side hustle to make some extra money. Though he is still far away from his goal, he now has the confidence to invest not only in the market but also in himself.

If this is you, here's a baby step you can take right now:

MICRO-ACTION: Pay a small amount to one debt. As Dave Ramsey says, pick the smallest debt you have and pay just a little bit. Next time you can, do it again, and maybe increase the payment by $50. Keep that momentum going!

BOUNCE THE BALL BEFORE YOU SHOOT IT

A LOT OF people come up with a great idea for making new friends: "I'll join the new basketball rec league!"

It's a great idea. But then the moment you show up, everything looks *much* more intimidating than what you had envisioned—everyone but you seems to know how this game is played, what shoes to wear, whom to pass to, all the rules, et cetera.

So, here's an idea: Before you join the basketball (or volleyball, or pickleball) league, go buy whatever ball you need, and just play with it for thirty minutes every night. Learn how to shoot, how to score. If you have a roommate or a spouse, practice with them. If you're by yourself, be creative—for baseball or softball, head over to the batting cages to hit some balls.

Sports are a lot less intimidating once you have some of the basics down.

> **MICRO-ACTION:** Go buy the equipment for the sport you want to learn, head to a park, and practice by yourself or with a roommate. As you get better, you can move on to the rec team.

HOW TO START YOUR OWN BUSINESS

I GOT THIS one from multimillionaire Noah Kagan, who's worked at Facebook and Mint and has started several businesses. He has a full business strategy that starts with this technique. Check it out in his *New York Times* bestselling book *Million Dollar Weekend: The Surprisingly Simple Way to Launch a 7-Figure Business in 48 Hours.*

Everyone wants to start a business. I speak with more and more people who want to, but they lack the confidence. Maybe they've given a few pieces of their artwork to friends, or maybe they've done a little yard work for free for the neighbors, and they think, *I enjoy this so much more than my day job, I should monetize it!* But starting your own business seems daunting.

- "How do I sell my product?"
- "Where do I get funding?"
- "How do I do accounting?"
- "How do I make money?"

Here's a great baby step you can take *right now:* Ask someone for your first dollar.

Literally text a handful of your closest friends with something like, "Hey, I'm starting a business . . . could you be one of the first people to support me by sending me a dollar?"

Trust me. Someone will send you a dollar to support you. Voilà—you've made your first dollar in your new business, which will give you confidence that someone actually believes in what you're doing, in who you are, *and* in your future company!

MICRO-ACTION: Text a handful of friends and ask if they could send you your first dollar for your new business. When someone does (and they will, believe me), post it on your wall as the first dollar you made in your business. Now you have a business.

HOW DO I MAKE NEW FRIENDS?

IN CHAPTER 2, we talked about Alex, who wanted to become a social butterfly, but during COVID, she'd actually become the opposite—a hermit. When everyone started getting back to their normal lives after the pandemic, Alex had withdrawn to the point she had full-blown social anxiety. So, she just started by taking her work to her favorite coffee shop every day.

Nothing difficult, just simple: Grab your laptop and head to the coffee shop to work. The trick is to show up at the same one for a while. You don't even need to have enough confidence to talk to anyone; that will probably happen naturally after you get to see who's a regular. If nothing else, the baristas will get used to you!

This trick is effective for students, for people who work at home, and even for people with typical office jobs. If you're in the last category, you can grab your favorite book and just hang out after work for thirty minutes or so. Trust me, it works!

MICRO-ACTION: Bring your laptop (or book) to the same coffee shop for a couple of weeks until you start to notice the regulars. Then find something easy to talk about to help you start up a conversation. You're on your way to making friends!

GO WHERE THE GIRLS (OR GUYS) ARE

ONCE, A YOUNG LADY whom we'll call Michelle was complaining about the lack of men in her world. Then her friend asked her where she was spending all her time. Michelle was a professional stage dancer. She spent all her time onstage or at ballet class. Guess how many guys were in her ballet classes? (If you guessed more than zero, you're wrong.)

Luckily, her friend gave her some advice. He told her to start hanging out at Home Depot. (It turns out he may not have come up with this idea on his own—I later heard that Brazilian fashion model Brittany Hugoboom [formerly Brittany Martinez] made the same suggestion to single ladies on her Twitter account.)

Anyway, Michelle did. She actually took a woodworking class. No dates from that class, but maybe she learned something, because she got into house-flipping and along the way met the man who would become her husband. Today she's married with children!

Sound ridiculous? Maybe, but if you're looking for a guy, try somewhere the guys are hanging out. (And vice versa if you're looking for a lady—ever try Pilates?) You don't need to ask anyone out on a date; you just need to show up.

MICRO-ACTION: Show up at a class, a store, a coffee shop, or someplace else where the people you want to date are likely hanging out. You don't have to go with the intention of finding a date immediately. Just be in the environment!

HOW DO I FIND THE BRAVERY TO JUMP BACK INTO DATING?

I HAVE A good friend we'll call James. He had an incredible thirteen-year-old daughter but, unfortunately, after a lot of fighting, his wife left them to start a new life with someone else, and James is now an older single man. To say his confidence was shattered would be an understatement.

How do you get some mojo back in the romance world, especially as a single parent? How do you find somewhere that's family-oriented?

Luckily, he received some amazing advice from his sister-in-law, who told him to join a local Bible study group. These places tend to be more family-friendly than a bar, and since the focus isn't technically dating, the pressure's off.

There are lots of ways you could probably re-create the group vibe—at a book club, at a recreational sports league, or by volunteering at your child's school. If you have a child, the trick is to find somewhere that has childcare or at least other people your kid's age so that your kid *also* can make friends, which helps the parents have the time to talk and connect.

MICRO-ACTION: Find one place—say, a Bible study group or gym class (one that offers childcare if you need it) and show up. Remember, put a date on it! As you attend, you'll inevitably figure out who has kids the same age as yours, and that's a good opportunity to strike up a conversation.

START WITH A "REVIEW"

TODAY, MANY PEOPLE want to get their creator on—with video content, a blog, or a podcast. But they often don't feel confident enough to get started.

- "How do I know my content is good?"
- "Will people like what I have to say?"
- "How do I find a good idea?"

Trust me—as a public speaker who has to maintain an on-line presence, I totally understand how hard it can be at first to come up with new content, and then to feel confident enough to post it. Here's an idea: Start off by reviewing other content. That way, you're just giving your opinion.

So, instead of writing a blog about ten outfits to wear in the fall, just look up what *other* people have said and post their ideas, giving them credit. Or, instead of making a podcast about a brand-new philosophy that you have, just make a podcast of you riffing on *All-In*, or Andrew Huberman, or Joe Rogan, or *Call Her Daddy*.

MICRO-ACTION: Publish your first post, blog, podcast, or YouTube video with a discussion of *someone else's* content. Do this a few times until you feel confident enough to branch out just a little and give your own thoughts.

CHANGE CAREERS BY ASKING THE EXPERTS

I KNOW A super-smart and capable woman who has an MBA and has run a successful business. She's primarily been a stay-at-home mom the last five years. She doesn't feel like she could re-enter the workforce, because she has been out of it for the last several years and feels like she's behind as far as experience goes.

If you're entering a new phase of life and you're ready to step back into the workforce, but you're quite intimidated, here's a baby step you can take right now.

Message twenty people who are working in the field you'd like to be in or who are in a job you'd like to have. Just say this: "Hey, I see that you're an expert in this. I'm wondering how to get into it."

Ask how they got to where they are. If that goes well, ask if there's a day you could come in and help them out with a project for free, just to see what they do that makes them so successful.

You may not receive a response, and maybe you'll even get a few nos. But after enough messages, you will get a yes.

So, whether you've been home with your kids or out of the workforce due to an illness or for any other reason and you're ready to step back in, take that little baby step.

MICRO-ACTION: Email twenty people this week and ask them how they got to be an expert in their job or field. When several of them reply, take their advice, put it on the calendar, and do it!

"MY FAMILY TREATS ME LIKE A KID"

I KNOW A WOMAN whose mother drives her up a wall. They have very different views on most things in life, and not only does her mother disagree with many of her choices, she also doesn't respect her boundaries. I think a lot of us can probably relate to this.

Instead of completely breaking off the relationship, this woman has chosen a wise strategy. She's tackling just one phrase her mom says often that bothers her. Often her mom will call and ask how her baby's doing (referring to her grandchild), and when that happens, she says, "Your baby's all grown up, Mom. But *my* baby is doing great."

If you're struggling to put some distance between you and your family, or if you want to do something they all think is crazy (like forgo a scholarship to MIT to pursue roles on Broadway), here's a baby step you can take right now.

MICRO-ACTION: Think of the one thing that person or group of people says that bothers you the most. Now come up with one phrase you can memorize and toss back every time they say that phrase. Voilà! You're on your way to being able to really stand up for yourself.

OVERALL: TAKE MESSY ACTION!

MAYBE YOU SAW yourself in the above examples, or maybe not.

Regardless, I hope one thing became very clear: Take messy action. No matter what you do, just try something. Point in the right direction *and go for it.*

It's OK if it blows up. It's OK if it feels like you didn't get far. Just go to the gym. Just smile and tell yourself, "Today's going to be a good day." Just push yourself to go a little further in confidence than you did yesterday.

Micro-Proof

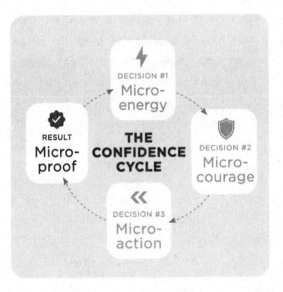

MICRO-PROOF: *A small piece of evidence that your confidence has evolved and your identity has changed, even just a little.*

Proof is the final step in a revolution around the Confidence Cycle. It's this little bit of evidence that allows you to begin a new cycle. Importantly, "proof" has much less to do with the outcome of an action, and much more to do with how you see yourself because you *did* perform the action.

If you're not confident that you can make new friends, and then you decide to invite a potential new friend to dinner, the proof occurs the moment you take action. Whether or not your friend says yes is up to them. Because you stepped out of your comfort zone and invited someone to dinner, you have shown yourself that you are capable of making new friends, even if this particular dinner date doesn't work out. That's *proof,* and if you allow it, that proof will give you enough energy to restart the Confidence Cycle.

9.

You Succeed
(Even When You Fail)

—

You don't become confident by shouting
affirmations in the mirror, but by having a stack of
undeniable proof that you are who you say you are.

—ALEX HORMOZI

WE'VE TALKED ABOUT BUILDING MICRO-ENERGY, A SPARK that gets you excited about what your future could look like. We've dug into micro-courage, the bridge that gets you from energy to micro-action. Micro-action is completing a small step that gives you proof that you're capable. And so, we arrive at the final stop in the Confidence Cycle: micro-proof. We can define micro-proof as a small piece of evidence that your identity has changed, even if just a little bit.

My friend Carter works at the Apple Store. As you know, this is a fast-paced, high-energy environment. Carter loves his job, but one part is just . . . *different.*

Every hour on the hour, Carter must deliver a presentation to the crowd of customers who've gathered in the store, demonstrating the latest Apple features and functions. It's pretty awkward, because everyone from the employees to the customers is busy doing something else—checking out gadgets, making sales, visiting the Genius Bar. Carter's presenting, and no one's listening.

Let's think about Carter's path to this moment. Maybe during his interview at the Apple Store, he learned he'd have to give presentations every hour of his workday. Maybe at first he felt nervous and wanted to look for a new job. But perhaps he decided that at the end of every workweek he'd reward himself by going to see a movie, big bucket of popcorn and all. Micro-energy. That energy gave him the boost he needed to take a small step toward being successful at his new job. Micro-courage. Maybe he decided to give the presentation to his friends and family before his first day on the job. This was a small step, but once Carter got through it, he felt that if he could give this presentation to people he knew, people whose opinions he actually cared about, he could certainly give this presentation to strangers. Micro-action. And that brings us back to our story.

No one's listening while Carter gives his presentation.

That's micro-proof of *something*. But what it's proof of is completely up to Carter.

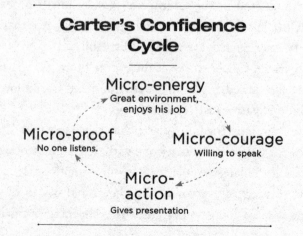

Carter's Confidence Cycle

Micro-energy
Great environment, enjoys his job

Micro-courage
Willing to speak

Micro-action
Gives presentation

Micro-proof
No one listens.

OPTION 1: Proof that Carter is bad at presenting because no one is listening.

OPTION 2: Proof that Carter has the confidence to present in a difficult situation and *keep moving forward.*

In *Batman,* Bruce Wayne is constantly asked by his dad, "Why do we fall down?" Young Bruce always answers: "To learn to pick ourselves back up." Falling down is proof not that you fell but that you can get back up and that falling doesn't kill you.

Carter gave the presentation, even though he didn't want to, even though it's uncomfortable. He's already won. He just needs to *choose* to see it that way. He needs to see the circumstances as proof that he can give a presentation no matter how difficult the circumstances.

Have you ever been skiing in a group? There's usually a less-experienced newbie who's terrified of the ski lift and of racing down the hill. But when they go up the lift and down the hill anyway, we all cheer for them *just because they did it.* Maybe they fell five times while going down the hill. That doesn't matter—they dealt with their fear and went for it. They can improve later.

That's why in the last couple of chapters, we talked a lot about simply taking action. It's not doing it perfectly that's the proof; the proof is *the action itself.* But we must consciously make that decision; otherwise the voices in our head will tell us, *See? You made a mistake. See? You didn't get an A on that test. See? A few people* did *laugh at you.*

But who cares? Most things have a pretty high forgiveness rate. (OK, maybe not skydiving or surgery.) You can get up onstage in front of a hundred people a hundred times and totally bomb, and as long as you claim it, you now have proof that you can speak in front of ten thousand people.

Sounds cheesy to you? Let's put it in a few real-life scenarios:

1. You have no confidence in your ability to complete a race. You energize yourself, have some courage, sign up, practice for a few months. Then you head to the 5K. Best-case scenario, you run faster than you thought possible, set a new PR, and place at the top of your bracket! Wahoo! Worst-case scenario, you drop out halfway. Guess what? You still signed up. You still practiced. You're still in better shape. You still ran 2.5K of a race. You still didn't die. All of that is proof, if you let it be, thus completing the Confidence Cycle and giving you energy for next time—when you'll probably come back and crush it.

2. You've been struggling with finding your voice at work. You finally decide that at the next meeting you're going to offer your suggestions. So, at the next meeting you raise your hand and offer up why you think the direction the managers are choosing can be improved. Best-case scenario, they think you're brilliant. Worst-case scenario, you'll step on some toes and someone may tell you, "Thanks, Dylan, but I think we'll stick with option A." So what that they didn't take your advice? You now have proof that you have what it takes to present an idea.

3. You own a business and you have to fire someone. This is going to suck. So, you do it. You let them go.

Best-case scenario, they say, "OK, I get it. This job wasn't for me anyway, but I appreciate the opportunity." Worst-case scenario, they cuss you out, cry in front of you, tell you it's their dream job, then post about it online. That won't feel good for a week or two. You may get a nasty comment or two in your DMs. Then, guess what? Everything will die down, and you'll have proven that you have what it takes as an entrepreneur, even if it's hard.

That's the reality we all have. Action *always works*, because it's proof in and of itself. *But* you do have to choose to see it that way, which brings us back to Carter.

Carter gives his presentation, nobody listens, and what does Carter do? Well, I've seen Carter do this (and it's pretty amazing). He gives every presentation with as much enthusiasm as humanly possible, regardless of what others are doing. Carter delivers like he is in front of a thousand screaming fans—even when his audience is a baby rolling around on the floor, a service dog barking, and not one person who finds his presentation interesting.

But think about it—who has more confidence than that? If you can give a presentation when no one cares, how much easier do you think it will be to do it when everyone's paying attention and loving it?

OUTPUT VERSUS OUTCOME

WHEN I GOT to college, I wanted to help others learn to deal with the same struggles I'd had growing up. If others also felt like they weren't good enough on their own, I wanted to inspire them to think otherwise. I wanted them to know that they weren't alone. The only problem was that this dream meant having to talk in front of people. Like, a lot of people. Anytime I thought about this, within moments every negative comment mean Mrs. H. had ever made came right back to me.

Well, I forced myself to call up Mrs. P., hoping she could provide another one-ounce mental boost. I asked her to help me speak at the high school she was now working at, and somehow she got them to agree. I was scheduled to give a one-hour presentation to a group of a thousand high school students. It petrified me, because who's more judgy than high schoolers? (The answer is no one.)

For weeks, I ran through my speech, going over every story again and again. When it was time for me to deliver my speech, guess what? I saw Mrs. P. standing in the back. So I took a breath, and took my next step. (Ten points for being someone's charger, Mrs. P.!)

I lost the audience within five minutes. It was one of those moments you see in movies where the room suddenly seems too small, the angle of the camera too tight. In the movie, this would have been when the bead of sweat slowly dripped down the side of my face.

I somehow managed to stumble through the rest of the fifty-five minutes, but it was the longest hour of my life. And I'm not proud of what I did next: I beat myself up about it for weeks.

But after some time passed, I thought back to what Mrs. P. had said: "You're really good, Juan, but you're being too hard on yourself." I let her words give me the *energy* I needed, and I booked another presentation. Then another. One was to a room full of a hundred seniors at seven in the morning, talking about who knows what. Another (my first paid gig) was at a vegan restaurant despite the fact that I *love* eating meat. Another was to a class of nine students where I talked about public speaking, even though I was still terrified of public speaking.

With every speech, the desire to get better came back like it had never left. I got addicted to it, knowing that another bit of confidence was on the other side of discomfort, of pain, of "nobody cares," of "we're falling asleep," of "we should have brought someone else in."

Notice what happened? Even though I didn't handle it super well (I beat myself up about it), it was still proof that I had spoken, because I had. It went terrible, and guess what? I'm alive.

It's insane to me how often our negative minds take the same information and misread it.

If you were on a hundred-mile bike ride and you got your tail kicked by some guy who's Lance Armstrong's brother, guess what? You were on a hundred-mile bike ride! That's incredible.

If your business is being sued for $12 million, guess what? Someone thinks you have $12 million.

This isn't Hallmark nonsense. It really works that way. Maybe you used to be a stunt performer and now you're fifty pounds overweight. Guess what? You've just proved that even overweight dudes have the ability to be stunt performers. Maybe you lost a million-dollar deal that you were *this close* to landing. Guess what? You got this close to landing a million-dollar deal.

Wade Eyerly, CEO of Degree Insurance, talks about this a lot. When he was sixteen years old, Wade lost a multimillion-dollar deal. Yeah, you read that right. He lost a multimillion-dollar business deal because someone cut him out, and Wade got nothing at all. In fact, he was broke afterward. For a long time, Wade thought he was a loser because of that. He was ashamed that he'd missed the opportunity, and he rarely talked about it. Later, though, he realized, "Dang. What sixteen-year-old makes it that far with a huge deal like that?" and he started swinging for the fences again.

He worked for the White House. Then as a spy (told you he was cool). Then he started an airline, and after that he invented college-degree insurance (they financially guarantee you'll make income commensurate with your degree).

One of my favorite ideas of his is pretty simple: You get almost the same benefit from attempting something difficult as you do for actually completing something that's difficult. In his upcoming book (which my team got a sneak peek of), Wade uses the example of an Olympic hopeful. Employers love hiring Olympic-level athletes because they're disciplined, hardworking people. But the difference between hiring an Olympian and someone who tried out for the Olympics is essentially nothing. To the employer, both being an Olympian and having tried out for the Olympics are proof of dedication, commitment, and work ethic.

I call this focusing on the *output* over the *outcome*.

The output is what you did, and no one can take that away regardless of how it went (the outcome). When you focus on the output, you recognize that you tried; you may (or may not) have "failed," but it's what you put in that matters. You can improve, iterate, and move on.

When you focus on the outcome alone, you only get to "win" when society says you win. And if you're only focusing on the outcome, then this can actually backfire: When you lose, it causes you to have less confidence:

- "I'm currently overweight, so I'm just an unattractive person."
- "I didn't get the promotion, because I don't deserve anything better than what I have."
- "The bank didn't like my business idea, so I'll never be an entrepreneur."

Focus on your *output*, not on the *outcome*.

THE SIGNALS WE GIVE OURSELVES

LET'S GO BACK to Wade Eyerly for a minute, the almost-teenage-millionaire turned White House employee turned spy turned serial entrepreneur. He talks a lot about "signaling," something I guess they teach you in spy school. Basically, signaling involves the (usually hidden) messages one party sends to another. For instance, if you wear expensive designer jewelry, you're signaling to those around you that you come from money, even if you don't say anything about your wealth. If someone speaks with an elegant hand twirl as they talk, that could be a signal that they are from high society.

Signals, importantly, are open to interpretation, because more often than not they aren't explicit. And Wade says that the most important signals are the ones we send ourselves.

You are sending yourself signals all day long. Every time you fail, succeed, almost succeed, or almost fail, you are sending messages about *who you are* and *what you do*. Importantly, you must read the signals correctly. Otherwise you can get them crossed. Here are a few areas I know of in which we most often misread the signals in our life:

The Signal	Misread Signal	How You Should Read It
I lost a lot of money.	I'm bad with money.	I'm finally noticing my spending habits.
I used to be better at this.	I'll never be good again.	I have the potential to get better, and I can prove it.
I'm out of shape.	I'll continually be in worse shape.	I have what it takes to be healthy.
I've tried this so many times.	I can't possibly get this right.	I'm a doer.
It didn't go the way I planned.	I'm not a good planner.	I had confidence, I tried, I failed, and everything's OK.

You can get really, *really* specific with these. Here's what mine could look like:

The Signal	Misread Signal	How You Should Read It
My running times aren't improving after six months of running.	I suck at running.	I'm a runner.
It feels like I've edited this chapter eight times already.	I can't write well.	I'm a writer.
I've moved three times in the last couple of years.	I don't have a home.	My home can be anywhere.
I still hate diving with sharks.	I still hate diving with sharks.	I *really* still hate diving with sharks.

Notice that the signals we tell ourselves ultimately impact what we believe about ourselves, as in our identity. This is especially true in the Confidence Cycle. Think about Carter. The signal he gets while presenting is "No one's listening to my speech." The misread signal might be "I'm bad at giving speeches." Instead, the signal should be "I'm great at giving speeches; even when no one's listening, I still have tons of energy!"

If we're trying to build proof, evidence that our identity is changing from someone who's unconfident and incapable to someone who is confident and capable, we need to make sure that the signals we're sending ourselves confirm that proof.

In the next chapter, I'm going to show the interplay between the proof and your identity.

For now, though, we've got to be able to take our losses and focus on the *output*, not the *outcome*.

A QUICK WORD OF
WARNING ABOUT WINS

IN THIS CHAPTER we focused a lot on the worst-case scenario. (Kind of ironic for a guy who spent a whole chapter telling you not to think negatively!) That's because most of us don't have a problem with realizing that success is proof that we're successful. Typically, the proof that we're good at something isn't the reason we need a boost of confidence. In other words, the even better news is that as we move around the Confidence Cycle, oftentimes the best-case scenario is a reality. If you do get up in front of everyone, they may love you. And in that case, you'll get a whole ton of energy to start your next Confidence Cycle—trust me!

The same is true with every win. You probably don't need a

chapter in a book to help you see why paying off debt, starting a successful business, landing an excellent job, and winning a date with that hot guy are all easily verifiable proofs that you should be more confident. However, I do just want to throw a little warning out there: If you only base your proof on wins, eventually you'll lose, and that will hurt.

There's a cool running app called Runkeeper, and on it, Coach Erin says something that's awesome: There's only one thing you need to do to prove that you're a runner, and that is to run.

Now, if you used only races you win to prove to yourself that you're a runner, you'd run into a problem. Eventually you'd lose, and then what? Your identity would take a beating. Instead of believing you were a runner because you practiced running, *you* thought you were a runner because you won races. No matter how fast you are, eventually you'll take an L. And that's true in every area of life. It's awesome to celebrate wins! You definitely should do that more. Just don't find your *identity* in winning. Find it in the output itself:

- You're a runner because you run.
- You're good with money because you save.
- You're a confident person because you try.
- You're a writer because you write.
- You're an entrepreneur because you have to check the box "self-employed" on your tax return.[*]

Micro-proof is the key that starts to unlock your new identity: a confident badass who's capable of doing anything. As

---

[*] Can you tell that it's near April 15 while I'm writing this?

you move from energy to courage to action to proof, you're showing yourself that you can do hard things. You don't have to do them perfectly, or fearlessly; you just have to do them. And once you get comfortable doing something that used to scare you—like giving presentations in the middle of a store while no one listens—you can expand your comfort zone and do things that are maybe even a bit scarier. You start back over at the beginning of the Confidence Cycle—you build energy, then you build courage, then you take action. You're able to do this because you've already *proved* to yourself that you *can* do it and you *did* do it.

And as you do that over and over again, your identity begins to change. You're becoming *confident.*

Confidence Cheat Sheet

- Focus on the *output,* not the *outcome.* You control the effort you put into a situation, and that should be your proof that continues the Confidence Cycle.
- When you decide to take action, there's a chance the outcome will be exactly what you feared. At this juncture you have a critical decision: Will you let the failure be proof that *you're* a failure, or will you take it as proof that even with the failure, you completed the action?
- We're constantly sending ourselves signals, and how we read them is up to us.
- Sometimes you win, sometimes you lose. That's not what determines your identity. You're a runner *because you run,* not because you *win.*

Micro-Step

For this chapter, I want you to write down ten of your most recent failures or mishaps. Then write down the two different ways to read that situation.

Here's a blank page to get you started. Or you can fill out an electronic copy at CONFIDENCECYCLE.COM /RESOURCES.

The Signal	Misread Signal	How You Should Read It

10.

From Micro-Proof
to Identity Shift

———

OVER TIME, WHEN STONE IS LEFT OUTSIDE, THE ELEMENTS alter its shape. What was jagged is now smooth to the touch; what was proudly silhouetted against the sky now merges into the surrounding landscape. And while the stone once stood tall despite the beating rain, now it slowly begins to surrender its individuality.

But what if, before its uniqueness is worn away, an artist finds the proud stone, takes it to their home, and begins to carve? A block of ordinary stone, full of imperfections, is carefully chipped away, piece by piece, until it is no longer just a stone. Now it's been shaped, bit by bit, into something *new*, something *intended.*

And that's exactly what you have the opportunity to do with your own identity: You can shape it, bit by bit. You do that with every revolution of the Confidence Cycle.

———

LUIS, WHOM I mentioned in the introduction, got a D-minus in English class. And that was a merciful grade. His instructor had pulled him aside to inform him that while she liked him, he wasn't a great student. She said, "I don't want to see you back here next year," so she gave him a D-minus. Without that grade, Luis wouldn't have graduated from high school, and likely wouldn't have gone to college.

But of course, his grades didn't improve upon arrival on a new campus. He eventually received a similar speech from his college professors: "We like you, but you aren't a great student. Take a semester off."

Luis was diagnosed with the big ADD—attention deficit disorder. Before taking the meds, he decided to research the condition and address the root problem. He started studying decks of cards. He read books on memorization. He began learning longer and longer sequences of numbers. He got good at memorization—so good that he started going to memory competitions. The kid who was terrible at school became a whiz. Then he started winning. He became a champion. Fox noticed and invited him on their TV show *SuperHuman*. There, among other things, at one point he memorized five hundred pieces of information (such as name and address) about a hundred different people, all within a day.

Not bad for a guy who was told that school wasn't his thing.

Now, for just a moment, think back to Chambliss's paper "The Mundanity of Excellence." He claims talent is a useless concept. Parents tell their children and teachers tell their students that talent is important, but they do this to encourage them to keep going, when in reality what it takes to surpass your competition is passion and consistent improvement. So if talent doesn't exist, why doesn't everyone become an Olympic swimmer? If the threshold for Olympic swimming is "so low as to be nearly universally available," as Chambliss wrote, what stops people from trying? Aside from the obvious answers of sacrifice, time, determination, focus, and so on, there exists an invisible wall, something I call the *identity threshold*, that traps each of us into a certain way of being. If a swimmer sees themselves not as an "Olympic swimmer" but just as an "average swimmer," they will cap themselves with a certain level of confidence, unable to ever push past it.

For some, the identity threshold may be "I'm not a reader" or "I'm socially awkward" or "I'm a lazy person." Each of these characterizing statements forms a cage around our confidence that feels impossible to break out of. For Luis, that looked like this:

- "I'm not good at school."
- "I'm not good at English."
- "I can't finish high school without some help from my teacher."
- "I can't finish college."
- "I have ADD."
- "I forget everything."

Eventually, all this seeped down into Luis's deep sense of himself, preventing him from getting past his own identity threshold. Even if he managed an improvement or two, that would likely not be enough to break through. This means that even if Luis started *energizing* himself with a new environment and other voices, having *courage* in school, and taking *action* toward better memory, giving him *proof* that he isn't dumb—in other words, if he went through a revolution of the Confidence Cycle—that wouldn't be enough for Luis, not even if he did it dozens of times. Each time would be better and easier than the last, but until that invisible wall of his old identity was shattered, he'd be vulnerable to falling back into his old negative patterns.

It can be hard to pinpoint when or how an identity threshold gets put into place. If you constantly tell yourself, "I'm a lazy person," were you born lazy? Of course not. So where along the journey did you pick up that identity? Conversely, you don't always know how many revolutions of the Confidence Cycle it will take to build a new identity.

Over the years, I've had several friends fall off their new habits, new behaviors, or confidence journey with no real explanation for why they didn't stick with it. They claim, "One day I just stopped doing it, and I haven't done it since." That's because their behaviors hadn't yet contributed to a new identity.

You break through your identity threshold the moment your micro-steps into confidence have fully transformed the way you see yourself (your identity).

Sure, I told you the goal of this book was to improve your confidence, and it is. But really, the bigger goal is to change your identity around the things you aren't confident in. You need to move from "I can't keep friends" to "I'm a good friend," from "I'm an overeater" to "I'm healthy," from "I'm bad in front of people" to "People enjoy listening to me."

Consider Mia. Mia was a star soccer player at her high school, but she lacked a close group of friends. Once she even told me, "I'm anxious about making friends. I don't think anyone's going to like me. What if I don't come off the right way? What if I'm awkward? What if no one wants to date me?"

Mia may have been a good soccer player, but she didn't

have a whole lot of confidence in her personal relationships. Regardless of what we would all call "proof" in her life—she was talented, beautiful, charming, smart—she didn't see it that way.

It wasn't until she took enough micro-action toward building relationships that her identity started to change. Once or twice wouldn't have been enough. She had to gain more and more proof of her ability to make friends until one day she *really* believed she was good with people.

Again, this is largely up to perception. If you truly believe that you're a hopelessly fat person, a run or two on a treadmill isn't going to shake that perception. In fact, even losing a few pounds—or, for that matter, all your excess weight—isn't necessarily going to change your life. You could take all the messy action in the world, which will inevitably help build your confidence, but if your identity deep down is rooted negatively in your belief that you're hopelessly overweight, one day, for some reason, you'll revert back to your old levels of confidence.

Sadly, many people do just that. They build what seems like confidence, and then they fall back into their old identity— because they never allowed their revolutions around the Confidence Cycle to actually reshape *who they are.* So, regardless of the evidence in front of them, they'll still see themselves as their old self.

For instance, if someone who has no self-confidence becomes a lawyer, but deep down they see themselves as a failure, a few wins here and there in the courtroom won't shake their deeply rooted core beliefs. They still may have no confidence, even though there's some evidence that they're actually *good* at what they do. For deeply rooted self-identity to change, you have to take a lot of spins around the Confidence Cycle.

So, to go back to the overweight individual: If they become confident that they are or can be a healthy person, guess what? Suddenly their confidence can help impact their actions:

- Healthy people go to the gym.
- Healthy people watch what they eat.
- Healthy people invest in their fitness.

In fact, healthy people can gain a few pounds, notice the trajectory, and turn it around. Why? Because they're healthy.

Your identity threshold can be different for different areas. If you have a deep-seated belief that you're bad at sports, it may take more than a few touchdowns to prove to yourself that you're wrong and rebuild your confidence. On the other hand, if you've never danced before but after a couple of classes you get a lot better, it may not take long for you to feel confident on the dance floor. There isn't a set number of revolutions of the Confidence Cycle that you need in order to positively impact your identity. The key is that once your identity *is* impacted, a deeper transformation occurs.

THE BATMAN EFFECT

IN 2017, RESEARCHERS released their findings from a child development study. The title of their research paper was "The 'Batman Effect': Improving Perseverance in Young Children."[1] (With a title like that, you *know* the information is going to be gold!)

The researchers asked young children to spend ten minutes completing what the adults thought would be for the kids a "long and boring" activity. Before starting, they told the young ones, "This is a very important activity, and it would be helpful if you worked hard on this for as long as you could." However, the children were allowed to quit the activity at any time if they felt it was too boring, and could instead play an iPad game (big stakes here, people).

The children were divided into three groups. The first group was instructed to think of themselves in the first person, and ask this question at prompted intervals: "Am I working hard?" The second group was to ask themselves, using the third person, "Is *Hannah* working hard?" The third group was to ask the same question in the third person, but not using their real identity; instead, they were told to imagine themselves as Batman, or a similar hero, and ask, "Is *Batman* working hard?"

(I've never been so excited to share results from a research study with anyone!)

The second group, the ones who distanced themselves from the activity by using the third person, lasted longer than the first. But—and this probably isn't surprising to you—the "Batman" group, the ones who took on a new identity, lasted the longest. Here's what the researchers wrote in their paper, with my commentary in brackets:

> Taking on the perspective of another person [especially the superheroes] could have [Could have? Nah, *definitely*!] provided the greatest separation from children's own experience, allowing them to disengage from immediate temptations or negative emotions and *focus on their goals*. . . . [Overall,] perseverance increased because children *identified with powerful features* of the characters they chose to impersonate.[2]

That's the power of identity. Importantly, nothing actually changed about the children; only their perception of themselves changed.

Are you hearing this? That's why, throughout this book, I've been hammering you (gently!) with ideas to get you to find energy, gather courage, take action, and find the proof you need. But in the end, your perception of all that determines how you translate it. That's why the proof must be examined, and why you must celebrate the wins—if you rush past the fact that you didn't go bankrupt after losing that business deal, or if you forget to acknowledge that today you didn't blow up at your spouse, or if you don't celebrate that you increased your sales close rate by a measly 5 percent, guess what? You are missing out on all the work you did. All of that is proof *only if you allow it to be proof.*

A colleague of mine, Matt, gives blood regularly now, and it's kind of embarrassing how proud he is of himself about it. He goes crazy about the fact that he's able to give blood. This guy is a successful entrepreneur, has written multiple books, and nearly set some world record on his 50 cc bike, but you'd swear his greatest accomplishment is the fact that he lines up, pulls up his sleeve, and sips apple juice a couple of times a year.

But he actually isn't bragging. He's excited because when he was younger, he nearly fainted the first time he gave blood. Well, he didn't give blood that day. They wouldn't let him. "Honey, you aren't giving blood today," they said to sixteen-year-old Matt. And that was it for Matt and giving blood—until his college friends pushed him into giving blood, with the strong encouragement of the watching eyes of a few college girls. (Matt shares this story so much, I swear I know it as well as he does.) Anyway, he shows up, sees the girls, and just prays that he doesn't faint. He doesn't faint, and he gives blood. The world has not changed much, but *he* has. And get this: After he gave blood for the first time, he found out that he's never had cytomegalovirus (CMV), which is a common virus most adults contract. CMV is totally harmless to them, but it can be lethal for babies. So now when he gives blood, they often put it in a special bag and call it "baby blood," telling him that his blood is special and will go on to save a baby's life.

His entire *identity* changed. Before, he was the guy who fainted trying to give blood. Now, he's the baby-blood guy. If you're the guy whose blood saves babies, think of how much more confident you are.

Once his identity shifted, his confidence grew tremendously.

IDENTITY CHECKPOINTS

EARLY ON IN my career, I obsessed over the best speakers in the industry. I studied how they talked, what they did with their bodies, what stadiums they spoke at. Eventually I noticed something they had in common: They had all spoken at the largest conference in the industry, the Super Bowl of conferences, the largest national conference in education in the United States. *Sixty-three thousand people.* I printed out a picture of that stage and taped it to my wall. Now, at this point I had only been speaking to classrooms of seven to ten people. But I knew that someday I would get on that stage.

A few years later, I was asked to speak in front of ten thousand people. At the time, I had only ever done a conference of a thousand people. But what did I say when they asked? "Absolutely, I can do that! Sounds great."

Cue a minor panic attack. *What am I doing? Can I deliver to that size crowd? Am I enough to handle it?*

Then it came time for the speech. I did my little energizer skip (see chapter 4), walked out onto the stage, took a breath—and confidently delivered my speech to an audience ten times larger than any I had ever spoken to before. It felt amazing. Then, a few days after that speech, I was approached about another.

"Hey, Juan, we'd love for you to speak at our state conference."

"Sure! If you don't mind my asking, how big is the stadium?"

"Maybe about five thousand people."

"Five thousand? Sounds great."This time *I actually meant it.*

I had broken through my former identity threshold, just like Matt. I was no longer the guy who "spoke in front of ten people." I'd gone around the Confidence Cycle enough times, and somewhere along the way I'd come to truly believe that I was the guy who spoke in front of thousands of people. Was I all the way to my audience of sixty-three thousand yet? No way. That would have freaked the heck out of me. But I'd reached a new era.

Life has its ups and downs, and people can say things about us that knock us back a few notches. Early in my career, I was told I was terrible—by Mrs. H., and even by a few clients. Guess what? That took a ton to overcome. At that point I was struggling with my identity as a speaker.

Over time, though, I grew. I moved the ball up the field. Maybe I wasn't on the goal line yet, but I'd reached a new era in my confidence. By that point, when I received bad feedback, it might upset me for a few days, or even fill me with doubt, but it didn't send me back to the beginning. It was like I'd lose a few yards, but I wouldn't wind up all the way back at the other end zone, like before.

What's cool about your identity evolving is that it really is like that adage "Two steps forward, one step back." If you keep at it, you'll reach a point where your self-doubt can push you back only so far. You have a new baseline level of confidence in yourself. Today, a mistake might cost you a night of stress, but no longer will it result in a week of stress.

It's like making progress in a video game. As you complete side quests, you hit checkpoints that save your place in the game. If you ever get killed or fail a challenge, you resume your progress at the last checkpoint you found, rather than going all the way back to the beginning. Our real-life goals work similarly. Each checkpoint is a micro-victory, a sign that shows how far you've come. It doesn't matter when you'll finish the game, or when you'll get to the final boss; what matters is the skills you harvest, the items you pick up, and the stamina you build. All of these things prepare you for whatever comes next.

Crossing the identity threshold is where one of the biggest battles in your life will come from. Here you're battling, hard, to overcome a previous perception of yours that you were a failure in some way. For me, it was perceptions like "Juan will never be good enough," "Juan can't write," and "Juan's just the fat kid." After enough effort—enough revolutions around the Confidence Cycle—eventually I shattered those beliefs.

Once I did, it became all about incremental gains at various checkpoints: "Juan won't always be fat." "Juan isn't as overweight as he used to be." "Juan may get healthier." "Juan is healthier." "Juan is in shape." "Juan is a Greek god of a man."*

Battle to find your new identity, then keep going at various new checkpoints.

OUR END, YOUR BEGINNING

SIX MONTHS FROM now, where will you be? What kind of person do you want to become?

When asked this question as a kid, I had no idea, as most people wouldn't at that age.

I asked that question of myself when I got friend-zoned by Brittany sophomore year. Again, I had no clue who I wanted to be. All I knew was the wave of rejection crushing me.

I didn't even bother asking myself this question when I was staring in the mirror, hating what I saw, wishing I had lived a different life, hoping something would come along to end it all.

One day, though, I caught a very brief glimpse of a different Juan. Someone who could speak without fear of judgment from others. Someone who didn't care about being perfect for anyone else. Someone who could swim with sharks and not die. Someone who could snowboard down the wrong side of a mountain and have the endurance and willpower to choose life. Someone who was *confident* in their choices about health, relationships, and well-being. That Juan was someone I was anxious to become.

Just one step.

Then another.

And a million more.

---

*   Gaby just rolled her eyes instinctually, without even reading this.

Each one easier and more confident than the last.

Until I was running.

Now, running is all I ever do.

Where you are now—how much or little is in your bank account; how successful your relationship is; how healthy your body is; where your mental health is—is a reflection of where your priorities, decisions, and commitments were six months ago. However much control or awareness you had back then doesn't matter; you're here now. Everything you think, feel, and do from here on out is up to you.

Before you shift gears toward the big moments, remind yourself to celebrate the small ones. Your confidence is built on your micro-victories; don't underestimate their importance. Without them, you'd have never made it this far into the journey.

So, looking at the next six months, what are the small one-ounce changes you need to make to bring you closer to who you want to be and the life you want to live?

We can't skip to the ending, so we might as well make the story interesting.

Confidence Cheat Sheet

- Good people often give up on their confidence journey because their *identity*—as an overweight person, as a person who "always" screws up, or as a general failure—never changed. Change the identity, change the behavior. Let the old identity live, and it will resurface.

- The identity threshold is the point at which you truly break through to a new paradigm. You've transformed from "I can't focus" to "I can focus," or from "I'll just always be bad with money" to "I can save money."

- Identity checkpoints are new baselines of your positive self-identity. Once you reach a new checkpoint, your baseline rises, and failures and mistakes can only push you back to that checkpoint, rather than sending you all the way back to the beginning.

Micro-Step

I want you to think about who you are *right now.* Has anything changed from when you started this book? Are there any fundamental beliefs about yourself that have changed? Maybe not; maybe, if you're honest, nothing has changed. That's fine, too. But if you recognize a belief about yourself that has fully transformed, write it down, and relish it: "My new identity is _____." That's big.

If you're not quite there yet, write down the identity that you want to have, and then, using a tool we learned from chapter 5, write down, "I don't quite fully believe this about myself, *yet.*"

Time to Open
the Door

———

S OMEDAY, MONTHS OR YEARS FROM NOW, AFTER YOU'VE finished this book and put it up on your shelf or lent it to a friend, there'll come a particular point in time, whether a significant moment in your life or a passing thought that catches your attention, when you will realize how far you've come. That where you dreamed of getting to, what you set out to do, who you decided to become has been done. That all the grinding steps, all the energy, courage, determination, and action, have led you to this instant. Maybe the difference is nearly imperceptible to others, but *you* know. You feel it.

Mine occurred when a good friend didn't recognize me after I'd gone through a period of weight loss and confidence transformation. It was a gathering of microscopic moments, a recollection of all the small choices I had made. Like a light going on in my head, that realization penetrated all the doubts associated with my old identity, and my once-threatening self-hatred evaporated like dew in the sunlight. I finally saw how different I had become.

Fast-forward to pursuing a publisher for this book. We received more than twenty rejections from different publishers, and it began to affect the confidence I felt in myself and what I believed in. But I knew this concept had the power to change lives. I knew what I had was special. So, we kept trying.

Eventually, we secured a book deal, and in the same week I received an invitation to be the opening keynote speaker at the giant stadium I'd pinned a photo of to my wall all those years ago, back when I was a twenty-year-old kid with a dream living in his parents' spare bedroom. I'm preparing for that speech as I write the pages of this book.

I still experience doubt, fear, and insecurity, regardless of how far I've come. The difference now is that I see those as the brightest indicators that I'm doing something right. I see my failures as opportunities for more energy. My every fear becomes an invitation for courage, every insecurity a chance to act with confidence. This is the Confidence Cycle.

So when those big moments come, and they will, my hope is that *you take them*. Without hesitation. If you're afraid, if you don't feel ready, if you feel like you're not good enough, remember who you are. Remember that the energy you need to overcome it all is already inside you. Remember the ten thousand steps it took to get you to this moment. The doubt, the fear, the uncertainty—they're just echoes of a past you've already outgrown. You have the power to open the unlocked door and step into your new life. So, take a deep breath and go for it. On the other side of that door is the extraordinary life you were always meant to live.

Acknowledgments

———

FIRST AND FOREMOST, I WANT TO EXPRESS MY DEEPEST GRATITUDE for everyone who made this book possible.

To the team—Josh Shipp, Paul Fair, Erin Niumata, Mary Reynics, Ivanka Perez, and others at Penguin Random House: Thank you for bringing this vision to life. Thank you for your guidance, expertise, patience, and for helping me shape this book into the most significant project of my career.

Thank you to my partners—the speaking bureaus, agencies, agents, managers, and mentors who have been instrumental in the impact I've been blessed to make.

To my clients: Thank you for placing your trust in me to deliver extraordinary experiences for your events over the years. I feel like the luckiest person in the world to have this career.

To my siblings, Sergio Bendaña and Adriana Bendaña: Thank you for believing in me from day one. Thank you for your inspiration and being the best role models I could ever ask for.

To my parents, Mami and Papi: Thank you for giving me an extraordinary childhood that shaped me into the person I am today. You are the reason for my work ethic, drive, compassion, and positivity. You sacrificed everything and left Nicaragua to build a better life for us, and I am so grateful for it.

To my friends—Nick Singh, Adam Johns, Stephen Szucs, Selina Raud, Matt Wallace, Taz Ahsan, Andrew Thomas, Luis Angel, Omid Kazravan: Thank you for always being there for me as I built my dream. When so many didn't believe in me, you did.

To my mentors—Tony Robbins, Brendon Burchard, Tom Bilyeu, Felix Lin, Michael Savage, Carolyn Sampson, Chuck Hogan, Marlon Smith, Scott Harris, Joseph McClendon III, Mel Robbins, Eric Termuende, Sarah Wells, Blake Fly, and Giovanni Marsico: Thank you for inspiring me to build a career out of helping people. It has been the biggest blessing of my life.

To the love of my life, Gabriela Bendaña: Thank you for believing in me more than I believe in myself. You have changed my life more than you will ever know. Thank you for believing in my dream, coming to the speeches in high school gyms, helping me craft stories, and being an integral part of developing the Confidence Cycle. I am so grateful to have such a thoughtful, kind, beautiful, driven, aligned, passionate, and loving soulmate to spend my life with. I can't imagine my life without you. I love you so much.

To Mrs. H.: Thank you for lighting the fire within me to become something people told me I could never become.

Lastly, to you, the reader: Thank you for your commitment to becoming the best version of yourself. You are the reason I wake up and show up with energy for my life. My hope is that after reading this book, you do the same.

Notes

———

1. CONFIDENCE IS A VERB

1. Adriana Malureanu, Georgeta Panisoara, and Iulia Lazar, "The Relationship Between Self-Confidence, Self-Efficacy, Grit, Usefulness, and Ease of Use of E-Learning Platforms in Corporate Training During the COVID-19 Pandemic," *Sustainability* 13, no. 12 (2021): 6633.

2. "Ed Sheeran," This Day in Music, May 21, 2024, https://www.thisdayinmusic.com/artists/ed-sheeran/.

3. Eveline Beck, "Ed Sheeran YouTube: How He Dominates Views & Clicks," Funktasy, May 18, 2023, https://www.funktasy.com/music-business/learn-3-ways-ed-sheeran-dominates-youtube/.

4. "Artist: Ed Sheeran," Recording Academy, https://www.grammy.com/artists/ed-sheeran/6178, accessed October 17, 2024.

5. "Ed Sheeran Had a Traumatic Childhood Due to a Medical Error," YouTube, posted by Vix, June 17, 2019, https://www.youtube.com/watch?v=70EyyOBkl_U.

6. "Ed Sheeran × Dave," YouTube, posted by Love Music Hate Racism, March 22, 2019, https://www.youtube.com/watch?v=woef-UeFtgQ.

7. Ed Sheeran and Phillip Butah, *Ed Sheeran: A Visual Journey* (London: Cassell Illustrated, 2017).

8. "Ed Sheeran," IMDb, https://www.imdb.com/name/nm3247828/, accessed October 17, 2024.

9. Sheeran and Butah, *Ed Sheeran,* 68.

10. George P. Hollenbeck and Douglas T. Hall, "Self-Confidence and

Leader Performance," *Organizational Dynamics* 33, no. 3 (2004): 254.

11. Ibid.

2. ONE OUNCE AT A TIME

1. Sean Saldana, "An Oral History of the Nike Cortez, 50 Years After Its Release," NPR, February 15, 2022, https://www.npr.org/2022/02/15 /1077040201/nike-cortez-50-anniversary-history-los-angeles.
2. "Nike Market Cap," Stock Analysis, https://stockanalysis.com/stocks/nke /market-cap/, accessed October 17, 2024.
3. Kenny Moore, *Bowerman and the Men of Oregon: The Story of Oregon's Legendary Coach and Nike's Cofounder* (Emmaus, PA: Rodale Books, 2006).
4. Phil Knight, *Shoe Dog: A Memoir by the Creator of Nike* (New York: Scribner, 2016), 44, Kindle edition.
5. Albert Bandura, "Self-Efficacy," in *Encyclopedia of Human Behavior*, ed. V. S. Ramachaudran (New York: Academic Press, 1994), 4:71–81. Reprinted in *Encyclopedia of Mental Health*, ed. H. Friedman (San Diego: Academic Press, 1998). Emphasis added.
6. Teresa M. Amabile and Steven J. Kramer, "The Power of Small Wins," *Harvard Business Review*, May 2011, https://hbr.org/2011/05/the-power -of-small-wins. Emphasis added.
7. Daniel F. Chambliss, "The Mundanity of Excellence: An Ethnographic Report on Stratification and Olympic Swimmers," *Sociological Theory* 7, no. 1 (1989): 70–86.

3. THE FIVE MICRO-ENERGY BOOSTERS

1. "Chemical Kinetics," Life Sciences 1A, Harvard University, https:// projects.iq.harvard.edu/files/lifesciences1abookv1/files/4_-_chemical _kinetics.pdf.
2. Jaime L. Kurtz, "Activation Energy: How It Keeps Happiness at a Distance," *Psychology Today*, July 10, 2016, https://www.psychologytoday.com /us/blog/happy-trails/201607/activation-energy-how-it-keeps-happiness -distance.
3. Amy Cuddy, "Your Body Language May Shape Who You Are," YouTube, posted by QuickTalks, June 26, 2012, https://www.youtube.com/watch?v= r7dWsJ-mEyI.
4. Tracy Brower, "Boost Productivity 20%: The Surprising Power of Play,"

Forbes, March 3, 2019, https://www.forbes.com/sites/tracybrower/2019
/03/03/boost-productivity-20-the-surprising-power-of-play/.

5. "Excessive screen time has been associated with increased levels of anxiety and depression and poor sleep quality." And "a brain overload could come as a result of the easy access to information through electronic devices and social media . . . [leading to] an increase in the production of the stress hormone, cortisol, as well as the fight-or-flight hormone, adrenaline, in response." Jasmin Elphic, "Stop Scrolling: How to Maintain a Healthy Relationship with Your Phone," St. Mary's Health Care System, July 20, 2022, https://www.stmaryshealthcaresystem.org/brand-journalism/blogs/stop
-scrolling-how-to-maintain-a-healthy-relationship-with-your-phone.

4.   HOW TO OVERCOME THE FIVE ENERGY KILLERS

1. Vijay Balasubramanian, "Brain Power," *Proceedings of the National Academy of Sciences* 118, no. 32 (2021): e2107022118, https://www.ncbi.nlm.nih
.gov/pmc/articles/PMC8364152/.

2. Elizabeth Scott, PhD, "Eustress Is the Good Type of Stress You Didn't Know You Needed," Verywell Mind, December 8, 2023, https://www
.verywellmind.com/what-you-need-to-know-about-eustress-3145109.

3. Brad Stulberg, "The Growth Equation: Stress + Rest = Growth," Medium, Thrive Global, May 31, 2017, https://medium.com/thrive-global/the
-growth-equation-stress-rest-growth-de95a5cdcd1d.

5.   "I'M NOT THERE, YET"

1. Farahnaz A. Wick, Abla Alaoui Soce, Sahaj Garg, River Grace, and Jeremy M. Wolfe, "Perception in Dynamic Scenes: What Is Your Heider Capacity?," *Journal of Experimental Psychology: General* 148, no. 2 (2019): 252.

2. Sean Howe, *Marvel Comics: The Untold Story* (New York: Harper, 2012).

3. "How Stan Lee Helped Revolutionize Comic Books," *PBS NewsHour,* aired November 16, 2018, https://www.pbs.org/newshour/show/how
-stan-lee-helped-revolutionize-comic-books.

4. Howe, *Marvel Comics.*

5. Stefanos Triantafyllos, "Heated Debate Around Antetokounmpo's Home Reflects Rift in Birthplace of Democracy," NBA Global, July 8, 2013, https://web.archive.org/web/20160610151612/http://www.nba.com/global
/antetokounmpo_center_of_heated_debate_greece_2013_07_08.html; Lee

Jenkins, "Freak Unleashed: Greek Freak," *Time*, January 3, 2017, https://time
.com/collection/american-voices-2017/4624632/giannis-antetokounmpo
-american-voices/; Matthew La Corte, "Giannis Antetokounmpo's Immi-
grant Story and the Internationalization of the NBA," Niskanen Center,
July 20, 2021, https://www.niskanencenter.org/giannis-antetokounmpos
-immigrant-story-and-the-internationalization-of-the-nba/.

6. JP Mangalindan, "Why Amazon's Fire Phone Failed," *Fortune*, September 29, 2014, https://fortune.com/2014/09/29/why-amazons-fire-phone
-failed/.

7. Austin Carr, "The Inside Story of Jeff Bezos's Fire Phone Debacle," *Fast
Company*, January 6, 2015, https://www.fastcompany.com/3039887/under
-fire.

8. Eugene Kim, "Amazon CEO Jeff Bezos Explains Why the Fire Phone
Disaster Was Actually a Good Thing," *Business Insider*, May 18, 2016,
https://www.businessinsider.com/jeff-bezos-why-fire-phone-was-a-good
-thing-2016-5.

9. Sonja A. Kotz et al., "Neuroanatomical Substrates of Continuous Adap-
tation to Cognitive and Communicative Demands," *Nature Communica-
tions* 10, no. 1 (2019); "Early Career Failures Can Make You Stronger in
the Long Run," Kellogg Insight, October 1, 2019, https://insight.kellogg
.northwestern.edu/article/early-setbacks-failure-career-success; David
Noonan, "Failure Found to Be an 'Essential Prerequisite' for Success,"
Scientific American, October 30, 2019, https://www.scientificamerican
.com/article/failure-found-to-be-an-essential-prerequisite-for-success/.

10. Noonan, "Failure Found to Be an 'Essential Prerequisite' for Success."

11. Erica R. Hendry, "7 Epic Fails Brought to You by the Genius Mind of
Thomas Edison," *Smithsonian Magazine*, November 20, 2013, https://
www.smithsonianmag.com/innovation/7-epic-fails-brought-to-you-by
-the-genius-mind-of-thomas-edison-180947786/.

12. Lucy Cox, "Gen Z's Military Malaise," *Berkeley Political Review*, February 27, 2024, https://bpr.studentorg.berkeley.edu/2024/02/27/gen-zs
-military-malaise/.

13. "Biographies: George Washington," National Museum of the United
States Army, https://www.thenmusa.org/biographies/george-washington/.

6. THE OPPONENTS

1. Alizabeth Lord Jetter, "A Qualitative Exploration of Courage" (MA the-
sis, Pepperdine University, 2010), https://digitalcommons.pepperdine.edu
/cgi/viewcontent.cgi?article=1080&context=etd.

2. Dorit Haim-Litevsky, Reut Komemi, and Lena Lipskaya-Velikovsky, "Sense of Belonging, Meaningful Daily Life Participation, and Well-Being: Integrated Investigation," *International Journal of Environmental Research and Public Health* 20, no. 5 (2023): 4121.

3. Jennifer Saibil, "Warren Buffett Predicted This Scenario, and It Could Play Out Again," The Motley Fool, June 16, 2023, https://www.fool.com /investing/2023/06/16/warren-buffett-predicted-this-scenario-and-it -coul/.

4. Pippa Stevens, "This Chart Shows Why Investors Should Never Try to Time the Stock Market," CNBC, March 24, 2021, https://www.cnbc.com /2021/03/24/this-chart-shows-why-investors-should-never-try-to-time -the-stock-market.html.

5. Saibil, "Warren Buffett Predicted This Scenario."

6. Justin Sablich, "How Scared Should You Be of Flying?," *New York Times*, August 10, 2017, https://www.nytimes.com/interactive/2017/08/10/travel /flight-safety-quiz-turbulence-american-airlines.html.

7. Daniel F. Chambliss, "The Mundanity of Excellence: An Ethnographic Report on Stratification and Olympic Swimmers," *Sociological Theory* 7, no. 1 (1989): 70–86.

8. Ibid. Emphasis added.

7. BABY STEPS ONLY

1. Eugene H. Peterson, *The Message: The Bible in Contemporary Language* (Colorado Springs, CO: NavPress, 2022), 1 Sam. 17:34–37.

2. MasterClass Staff, "Writing 101: What Is the Hero's Journey?," Master-Class, last updated September 3, 2021, https://www.masterclass.com/articles /writing-101-what-is-the-heros-journey#1NSljBEzxqOZEInrZJXwqp.

3. James L. Mandigo and Nicholas L. Holt, "Putting Theory into Practice: Enhancing Motivation Through OPTIMAL Strategies," *Revue phénEPS/ PHEnex Journal* 1, no. 1 (2009).

4. Paul Gwamanda, "Kobe Bryant and His Insane Work Ethic," Medium, October 16, 2020, https://paul-gwamanda.medium.com/kobe-bryant -and-his-insane-work-ethic-7c3e92094bc6.

5. Evan Andrews, "9 Things You May Not Know About Michelangelo," History.com, last updated August 7, 2023, https://www.history.com/news /9-things-you-may-not-know-about-michelangelo; "The Story of Michelangelo's David," Victoria and Albert Museum, https://www.vam.ac.uk /articles/the-story-of-michelangelos-david.

10. FROM MICRO-PROOF TO IDENTITY SHIFT

1. Rachel E. White, Emily O. Prager, Catherine Schaefer, Ethan Kross, Angela L. Duckworth, and Stephanie M. Carlson, "The 'Batman Effect': Improving Perseverance in Young Children," *Child Development* 88, no. 5 (2017): 1563–71.
2. Ibid. Emphasis added.

Index

A

"The A Team" (song), 7–8
action. *See* micro-action
activation energy, 52
Aladdin (film), 137–38
Amabile, Teresa M., 38
Antetokounmpo, Giannis, 96

B

Bandura, Albert, 35, 61
Batman Effect, 190–93
Bendaña, Juan
  background, ix–xi
  becoming a professional speaker,
    xvi–xvii
  communication skills, xii
  dissatisfaction with life, xii–xiii
  on failure, 35–36
  fitting in, xi–xii
  fresh start, xiii–xiv
  patterns of change, 28–29
  rejection experience, 108–9
  as a runner, 141–44
  seeds of the Confidence Cycle,
    xiv–xv
  shark diving, 103–5
  at Soul Cycle class, 35–36

Bezos, Jeff, 96–97
Blue Ribbon Sports, 21
Bowerman, Bill, 20–22, 26, 27, 53
bravery, through discomfort, 42
Bryant, Kobe, 149
burnout, 81
business, starting a, 158–59

C

Campbell, Joseph, 136
careers, changing, 163–64
celebration, as key to habit forming, 41
Chambliss, Daniel, 38, 126–27, 128,
    129, 130–31, 186–87
chargers, who build you up, 60–63,
    67, 78
comic books, 93–94
competence, 9, 12–14, 36, 140
confidence
  definition of, 16, 19
  as a practice, 15–16, 17–18
  as a skill set, 13–14
confidence building
  acceptance of, 41–42
  defining, 39–40
  examples of, 27–28

confidence building (*cont'd*)
Fogg's one little tooth, 24–26
Goldilocks step, 39–41
possibility of, ix
purpose of, 22–24
secret of, xix–xx
success fueling next attempt, 26–27
Confidence Cycle
action (*See* micro-action)
courage (*See* micro-courage)
development of, xiv–xv, xviii
energy (*See* micro-energy)
example of, xix
examples of, 30–34
overview, 29–30
power of, xx–xxii
proof (*See* micro-proof)
confidence journey, 139–40
confidence noun, 15–16
control, of your confidence, xviii, 5, 14–15
Cortez, the (shoe), 21
courage. *See* micro-courage
criticisms. *See* negative thoughts
Cuddy, Amy, 55

D
dating, micro-actions for, 160–62
David and Goliath (story), 135–36
DC Comics, 93
debt control, 156–57
decision-making, 119
discomfort, xiv–xv, xix, 27, 30, 42
Disney, Walt, 95
drainers, 60, 78–80

E
economic realities, courage facing, 47–48
elite swimmers, 126–27
energy. *See* micro-energy
energy killers
burnout, 81
drainers, 78–80

navigating, 78–79, 86
negative thoughts, 72–75
overview, 69–70, 85–86
poor habits, 75–77
stress, 80–81
toxic people, 78–79
toxic physical environments, 70–72
energy sparks, 52–53, 84
environment, power of, 70–72
eustress, 80–81
excitement, micro-courage and, 26–27
excitement anchors, 58–60, 66
exercise, micro-actions for, 154–55
extremism, 99–100, 118–19, 139
extroversion, 9–10
Eyerly, Wade, 175–76, 177

F
failures
creating stories from, 92
equals success, 98
extremism with, 99–100
human condition as story of, 97–98
as opportunities, 200
of real-life heroes, 95–97
reframing, 98–100
of superheroes, 94–95
as unavoidable, 106
family relationships, 164–65
fear(s)
courage coexisting with, 111–13
impacting decision-making, 119
of inadequacy, 113–14, 125–30
navigating, 112, 115–16
overview, 113, 130
of rejection, 113, 114–16
taking us to the extreme, 118–19
of the unknown, 113, 117–24
Federer, Roger, 124–25
feedback, bad, 194–95
financial control, 156–57
Fogg, BJ, 24–26, 28

Four Confidence Myths
  competence, 12–14
  debunking, 19
  extroversion, 9–10
  genetics, 11–12
  zero insecurities, 10
friends, making new, 159–60

G
genetics, self-confidence and, 11–12
Goldilocks step, 39–41

H
habit(s)
  of constant challenges, 127
  key to forming, 41
  poor, 75–77
  reaching goals with, 77
Hall, Douglas T., 13, 14–15
Heider, Fritz, 91
heroes, 3, 93–97
hero's journey, 136–38
Hollenbeck, George P., 13, 14–15
Hugoboom, Brittany, 161
human condition, failure as story of,
  97–98

I
identity
  Batman Effect, 190–93
  changing one's, 189–90
  determining your, 180–81
  evolving, 194–95
  falling back to old, 189
  overview, 197
  perception of, 192–93
  power of, 190–93
  shaping your, 185
  unlocking your, 180–81
  in winning, 180
identity checkpoints, 193–96, 198
identity threshold, 187–90, 194–96,
  197–98
I'm not there, yet, 99–100, 107

inadequacy
  fear of, 113–14, 125–30
  worries over talent, 127–29
innate strength, 11
insecurities, 10
introverts, 10

K
Kagan, Noah, 158
Kellogg School of Management,
  97–98
King, Stephen, 96
Knight, Phil, 22
Kramer, Steven J., 38

L
Lee, Stan, 93–94

M
Magness, Steve, 63
Mandigo, James L., 140
Martell, Dan, 83–84
Michelangelo, 151
micro-action
  for career changes, 163–64
  for dating, 160–62
  debt control, 156–57
  defining steps, 145–47
  definition of, 30, 140–41
  examples of, 31–34
  exercise and, 154–55
  family relationships and, 164–65
  finances, control of, 156–57
  making new friends, 159–60
  messy vs. no, 141–44, 165
  overview, 133–34
  progress on (*See* progress)
  for social media content, 162–63
  sports participation, 157–58
  starting your own business, 158–59
  toward building relationships,
    189
  when no one is watching, 150–51,
    152

micro-courage
  connection between excitement
    and, 26–27
  definition of, 30
  examples of, 31–34
  fear coexisting with, 111–13
  overview, 89–90
micro-energy
  activities to increase, 50
  anticipation of the future and,
    47–48
  based on previous failures,
    120–21
  boosters (*See* micro-energy
    boosters)
  byproduct of, 46
  chargers, 60–63, 67, 78
  creating, 42
  definition of, 30
  drainers of, 60, 78
  examples of, 31–34, 49–51
  excitement anchors, 58–60, 66
  introduction to, 48–53
  little sparks of, 52–53, 84
  overview, 110
  physical posture impacting, 55–57
  power of, 83–84
  skipping routine, 54, 55–56, 194
  starting Confidence Cycle with,
    xv–xvi, 34–35
  strong "why," 67
micro-energy boosters
  childlike activities, 57
  customized rest, 63–65, 67
  fixing physical posture, 54
  posture pick-me-ups, 55–57, 66
  strong "why," 65–66
micro-improvements, 129
micro-proof
  action as, 171–73
  definition of, 30, 169
  examples of, 31–34, 169–71
  failure as act of, 35–37

keeping promises to yourself
    as, 77
  output vs. outcome, 173–77, 181
  overview, 35, 167–68
  signals as confirmation of, 179
  unlocking your identity, 180–81
micro-victories, 195, 197
Miller, Donald, 92
monomyth, 136
motivation. *See also* willpower
  enhancing, 140–41
  examples of, 51–52
  lack of, 83
  making progress as, 38
  proof as, xix

N
narrative, framing the, 101–5
"navigate, don't eliminate" strategy,
    78–79, 86
negative thoughts, 72–75
Nike, 21–22

O
Obama, Barack, 9
opponents, making friends with,
    130
output vs. outcome, 173–77, 181

P
perfectionism, 138–41, 152
Peterson, Jordan, 70
physical posture, impacting energy,
    55–57
play, as key ingredient to learning/
    productivity, 57
posture pick-me-ups, 66
predictions, 119–21
proactive thought, 106–7
progress
  celebrating small, 148–49, 152
  defining steps, 145
  enemy of, 138–41

realizing how far you've come, 199–200
sense of, 38
value of, 145–47
proof. *See* micro-proof

R
Ramsey, Dave, 157
Randall (case example), 32–34
rejection
   author's experience with, 108–9
   fear of, 113, 114–16
   as painful, 114
relationship-building, 189
rest
   customized, 63–65, 67
   as intentional, 64
   proactive, 64
rest and recovery, 81–82
rituals over reasons, 76–77
Robbins, Tony, 55
rubber-band trick, 74–75

S
self-confidence
   academic studies on, 4
   control of, xviii, 5
   need for more, 3–4
self-confidence score, 4–5
self-doubt, 10
self-identity. *See* identity
self-limiting beliefs, xx–xxiii
self-reinforcing cycle, as path to self-confidence, 29
Sheeran, Ed
   background, 6
   disproving Four Confidence Myths, 8–9
   fueling next attempt, 27
   life as a pattern, 16
   music pursuit, 7
   social anxiety, 111

stuttered speech, 6–7
"The A Team" (song), 7–8
signals/signaling, 177–79, 181
Simmel, Marianne, 91
skipping routine, 54, 55–56, 194
social anxiety, 25, 31, 111, 159–60
social media audit, 75
social media postings, micro-actions for, 162–63
sports participation, 157–58
stories/storytelling
   framing the narrative, 101–5
   humans hardwired to create, 91–92
   reframing your flaws, 93–99
strengths, focus on, 126
stress, 80–82
Stulberg, Brad, 63
superheroes, holding ourselves to higher standards than, 93–94

T
talent
   as useless concept, 186–87
   worries over, 127–29
thoughts, power of own, 72–75
toxic environments, 70–72
toxic people, 78–79

U
unknown, fear of
   decision-making impacts, 119
   extremism and, 118–19
   introduction to, 113
   letting go of failures, 124–25
   overview, 117–19
   predictions and, 119–21
   stock market analogy, 120, 121
   strategies for, 121–24
U.S. Navy SEALs, 99

W
Washington, George, 101
weaknesses, 126

Williams, Jay, 149
willpower, 45–46, 49–51
Winfrey, Oprah, 95
wins/winning
  finding identity in, 180
  warning about, 179–81

words, power of, 61–63
workplace
  changing careers, 163–64
  confidence in the, 13

ABOUT THE AUTHOR

———

JUAN BENDAÑA is a highly sought-after speaker, entrepreneur, and coach to CEOs, Olympians, Grammy
Award–winning artists, actors, and Fortune 100 leaders.
Over the past decade, he has built high-impact leadership programs for companies such as Disney, American
Express, Zillow, and countless others. He has empow-
ered over 250,000 leaders in person—and reached millions more online—with a mission to help people build
unshakable confidence and take bold action in their
lives and careers.

Bendaña has been called "a walking shot of espresso"
for his contagious energy and is proof that confidence
isn't something you're born with—it's something you
build.

juanbendana.com

Instagram: @juanbendana

YouTube: @JuanBendana

LinkedIn: Juan Bendana